Nine Mile Magazine
Spring, 2023
Vol. 11, No. 1

NINE MILE MAGAZINE

Publisher: Nine Mile Art Corp.
Editors: Bob Herz, Stephen Kuusisto, Andrea Scarpino
Associate Editors: Cyrus Cassells, James Cervantes, Norman
Dubie, Christopher Merrill, Pamela (Jody) Stewart
Cover Art: From a montage "Scherzo 6" by Elena Ciletti.

Nine Mile Magazine is an imprint of Nine Mile Art Corp.

The publishers gratefully acknowledge support of the New
York State Council on the Arts with the support of the
Governor and the New York State Legislature. We also
acknowledge support of the County of Onondaga and CNY
Arts through the Tier Three Project Support Grant Program.
This publication would not have been possible without the
generous support of these groups. We are very grateful to them
all.

ISBN: 9798374711424

Contents

About Nine Mile Magazine

We publish twice yearly, showcasing the best work we receive from authors whose work, energy, and vision seem to us most deeply entangled with life. This includes writers within and outside the mainstream, writers with disabilities, writers of color, writers with marginalized genders and sexual orientations, and writers from different cultures and religions. We produce this magazine in inclusive and accessible formats. We believe that poetry is everyone's art.

Submissions

For consideration in the magazine, submit 4 - 6 poems in Word or text to editor@ninemile.org. You can access a submission form at our website, ninemile.org. Please include:
- your name and contact information (email and home address for sending contributor's copies),
- a paragraph about yourself (background, achievements, etc.),
- a statement of your aesthetic intent in the work,
- a photo headshot of yourself.

If you do not hear from us within two weeks, reconnect to make sure we received your submission. Note that we do not accept unsolicited essays, reviews, video / motion based art, or Q&A's.

Talk About Poetry podcasts and blog

At our Talk About Poetry podcast, working poets discuss poems that interest, annoy, excite, and engage them. The Talk About Poetry blog provides more opportunities for feedback. The addresses are:
- -Soundcloud: https://soundcloud.com/bobherz;
- -iTunes: https://itunes.apple.com/us/podcast/talk-about-poetry/id972411979?mt=2;
- -Talk About Poetry blog: https://talkaboutpoetry.wordpress.com.

Nine Mile Books

Nine Mile Books are available at our website, www.ninemile.org, or online at Amazon.com. Recent books are:

- *This Momentary World*, Jody Stewart, $16. "For over forty years now, I have followed with great admiration the career of Jody Stewart. She aligns herself to the tradition of those essential Middle Generation poets, Bishop and Jarrell. She possesses something of Bishop's acuity of seeing and hard-won sense of wonder, and something of Jarrell's narrative complexity and recognition of heartbreak. Stewart has also hewn a style that is all her own, notable – among other things – for its startling enjambments, its idiosyncratic but exacting approach to syntax, and its haunted (and singular) music. This generous selection, drawn from five decades of work, represents contemporary poetry at its very best." —David Wojahn, author of *World Tree* (2011)

- *Inside the Invisible*, Daniel Simpson, $10, Propel Poetry Award winner. "Simpson's poems propose that musicality should strive toward making sense—of losses, of small or large discoveries, of the very business of inquiry. There is even comedy in this as the poet meditates on what takes the place of literature in the lives of those who don't read it: *Let us pray for poetry / that begins in love / and then moves outward. / May it fill the mouths / of all who love.*" — Steve Kuusisto, from the Introduction.

- *Creating the Faces and Other Poems*, Tito Mukhopadhyay, $10. Propel award selection. "Tito Mukhopadhyay has been a pioneer in disability poetry over the past decade. In *Creating the Faces and Other Poems* he writes assuredly about what he does not know and skips customary "likeness" for freshness. Seeing a man with reading glasses on a bus he says: "I was relieved never to know his face. Looking directly at a human face is not easy for me. Faces blur or begin to turn into something else every time I try to look. I preferred a pair of reading glasses reflecting through the window - how the outside reflected back through the reflection."— Steve Kuusisto, from the Introduction.

- *Swoon*, D.J. Savarese, $10. Propel award selection. "DJ Savarese's poetic intelligence is alive and capacious and generous. These poems range from the small and daily to the grand and luscious, but every one is marked by devotion to the individual moment and tenderness for lived experiences, even the painful ones. Every realization is unexpected and new, every brightness forgiving, every darkness a new chance to understand. I am simply in awe of such a keen eye, such a musical ear, such a golden construction of attention." — Kazim Ali, author of *Sukun: New and Selected Poems* (Wesleyan University Press, 2023)

- *Bad To Me,* G.M. Drosdowich, $16 on Amazon. "Not a memoir or a remembrance exactly, but something better: a book true to the time and events it describes, and the characters who actually lived these late 60's college days, when finding and losing yourself in the endlessly unsatisfying quest for authenticity and its semi-attached furies of sex and innocence, were how we lived, fought, doubted, and loved."—Bob Herz, editor of *Nine Mile Magazine* and of *The City*.

- *The Burning Boat*, Linda Pennisi, $10. "'Ballerinas do not lose control; they shape grief,' begins one of the many stunning poems in Linda Pennisi's The Burning Boat, 'What do you think the positions are for?' How well these poems know that, gracefully stretching memory into shape after evocative shape: into a house that 'cannot stop thinking…of the Jesuses it held / on its walls,' into 'angels rearranging / the sky around their wings,' into ghosts 'as dense as ultrasound shadow…as ethereal as fetal dreams.' Pennisi's sense of metaphor—

sometimes subtle, sometimes startling—never disappoints. 'Your words, once spoken, forge a path for you' claims one poem. The Burning Boat forges many such paths, all worth walking again and again. —Philip Memmer, author of *Cairns* and *Pantheon*

- *The City*, by Bob Herz, $10. "It's remarkable how cohesive these poems remain throughout, or what a truly remarkable intro poem the first one is, as the first line serves as the powerful and knowing key to unlocking the entire theme. 'I came back to my city to feast with death.' And so it had me from that moment on! There is a steady, almost haunting undertone of drollness incorporated into the many deceptively awful things that recur in everyday life; how they flower and go to seed in the course of this thin but rich volume. And by the time I reached and entered the final poem, 'For the Day After Election,' I was struck with the almost gleeful despair of the narrator. As one of the 'poor wandering bastards' of the remaining world, I looked into my mirror and I read the seismic future aloud.—Sam Pereira, author of *True North and Untrue You*

- *Ceruleana*, by Caroline Manring, $16. "Ceruleana is filled with a charged stillness that I have only felt before as a child, when a hurricane's eye finally arrived and I walked out of the boarded-up house to wonder at my small, quiet, broken world. These poems stumble forward, curl back on themselves, crack apart, crack jokes, embodying both that brokenness and the strength we find to survive it. Caroline Manring has written a beautiful and heartrending book that proves her hypothesis: 'layers / of pain like / paint make / luminosity.'"–Dan Rosenberg, author of *Bassinet and cadabra*, winner of the American Poetry Journal Book Prize

- *Dog or Wolf*, by Bill Schulz, $10. "Given that one of Bill Schulz's keenest subjects is loss—the ongoing subtraction of people we've loved, places we've lived, moments when life has ensorcelled us—his poems are nonetheless remarkably joyful. And given that a signature feature of his style is a Zen-like kind of exacting minimalism, the poems nevertheless abound with the creatures and charms of the natural world. Reading Schulz is a bit like hiking the narrow road to the deep north with Basho at your left ear and Wallace Stevens at your right. It's a trip you do not want to miss!"— Jim Crenner, author of *Drinks at the Stand-up Tragedy Club*

- *green girl*, by Jessie Sobey, $16. "Harrowing, vertiginous, haunted, the poems in green girl excavate the image of Ophelia, fracturing her into prismatic bits— sister, self, drowned, undrowned, resurrected, never-dead, survivor and ghost, the one who's been silenced and the one who speaks. This fierce book interrogates the idea that 'I am not what I am' in ways that linger, challenge, and disrupt."—Laurie Sheck

- *Manual Random Hill*, by Patrick Williams, $16. "Many books talk about the impact of technology and media on our daily lives, but few give us new ways of finding human ground through technology and media. Manual Random Hill, Patrick Williams' remarkable debut, delivers tight, nostalgia-free poems about an analog world slowly weaving itself into the digital fabric of our daily lives. Williams reveals intellectually sharp, intimate and deeply human shapes hidden in the seemingly mundane interactions of our screen-focused and off-screen lives. The poems work to deftly remediate the constant presence of data around us and remind us that 'You & I are merely squatters/on the tiniest parcel of joint and muscle/pain.' Manual Random Hill is a remedy we sorely need."—Sean M. Conrey, author *of The Book of Trees* (Saint Julian Press, 2017)

- *Liminal*, by Bill Burtis, $16. "This is the world of real relationships, real children, real history, real joys and failures, inhabited by real owls and bats and coyotes, along with real stands of sugar maple and pine groves, snowy mountains and woodland ponds. These poems effectively ease you over that threshold to the world of what-if and if-only, the realm of existential pondering and deep interrogation of the self, the territory of nightmares of regret and visions of resolution, poignant dread and soothing hope. Burtis's poems always transport you to such a threshold to make you feel you are about to learn to fly, and fill you with that rare joy that only real art can conjure."—Jim Crenner, author *of Drinks at the Stand-Up Tragedy Club*

- *Someone Falls Overboard*, by Steve Kuusisto and Ralph James Savarese, $16. "Who hasn't wanted to live that writer's dream, eavesdropping on two great poets? For nine days, Steven Kuusisto and Ralph Savarese exchanged poems, multiple poems daily, and responded to each one: riffing, sampling, griping, cracking wise. The result is Someone Falls Overboard: Talking Through Poems, a project suggested by the poetic dialogue between William Stafford and Marvin Bell, but unmistakably Kuusisto and Savarese. Water runs through this book: a paradise, a poem-drinker, a physical place where the poets boat together, 'Two disabled men—this isn't a joke,' on Lake Winnipesaukee... Someone Falls Overboard is crackling smart, hilarious without losing its urgency, centered firm in this historical moment yet an instant classic in the long tradition of poetry in conversation. Reading is listening, ear pressed against an irresistible door."—Susanne Paola Antonetta, author of *The Terrible Unlikelihood of Our Being Here*

- *The You That All Along Has Housed You: A Sequence*, Leslie Ullman (2019), $16, or $9.99 at Kindle and iBooks. "Leslie Ullman has the ability to spin illuminating spells through and around the matter of earth and life. Her vision penetrates with an attention as careful and as transforming as day through clear water, as moonlight on stone. She is an artisan with words, and the results are poems embodying the intricacy and beauty of the subjects they honor." —Pattiann Rogers

- *Last Poems of Jules LaForgue* (2020), translations by Bob Herz, $10. "He is an exquisite poet, a deliverer of nations … a father of light" — Ezra Pound "…he was a liberating force, in style and form and subject matter... he encouraged a number of American poets to speak with greater freedom, in voices that later proved to be their own." — Malcolm Cowley
- *Last Poems of Georg Trakl* (2021), translations by Bob Herz, $10. This book includes all the poems Trakl wrote in the last two years of his life, from Sebastian in Dream and the poems that appeared in Der Brenner.
- *Some Translations*, by Bob Herz, $10. Translations with introductions that have previously appeared in Nine Mile Magazine, and in Nine Mile Books: Apollinaire, Trakl, LaForgue, Dante, Eluard, many others.

From the Editors

Welcome to *Nine Mile Magazine* Vol. 11 No. 1—a new decade begins! This is exciting, and to be honest, almost a surprise. We began as an online magazine, with no great hope that we would last beyond an issue or two. But within a couple years we began a print version, then a book series, a podcast, and a blog. It all seemed so natural, and almost an inevitable progression from one activity to the next!

It is also exciting, on the verge of this new decade, to look back and see the work we have published, everyone from Marvin Bell to Sandra McPherson to David Lloyd to Liz Libbey to Jasmine Bailey, and a hundred or so for whom there is not enough room here to name; and of course, also our special issues, anthologies of great younger poets, or of disabled poets.

Our format has been different than other journals from the start, because we wanted a way of showing poetry that would be helpful to the reader. With each selection we include a picture of the poem, and a brief bio, and also remarks by the poet as to what he or she is up to in these poems. We believe it helps to locate the reader with respect to the poetry being read, and that it creates a more sympathetic bond between work and reader, establishing the grounds for a better reading experience. And we have developed what have become the most popular sections of the magazine: the Appreciations & Asides section, and the extended sheaf of poems by a single poet that opens the issue.

It is impossible, of course, in a poetry world as fragmented and fraught as ours is, to publish every good poem sent our way, or to avoid turning down poems of quality. But we set out to accomplish a couple of things: one was to publish the best poetry sent to us (different than the best poetry in the world at that time), and a second, to respond to submissions quickly, within a week or two, an important goal, as all of the editors of this magazine are working poets and have felt the scourge of long holds of our poems by reputable magazines—sometimes a year or more. We believe that this new issue continues that promise of excellence to readers and expedited decision making to authors.

This issue is full of earthly delights: The poems by Doug Anderson show why so many of us revere him as a poet, and the sheaf of protest poems against other magazines' gag order on publishing on social media is fun and appropriate. There is also the brilliant piece by James Cervantes, "Commedia dell'arte," and David Weiss' stunning pieces on Chekov, Martin Willitts's wonderful "Hayden's The Last Seven Words of Christ" and our translations of the stunning poems of Robert Desnos.

With this issue we also announce the first three poetry books by three disabled writers. They are brilliant books, the first of the series to be published annually in each of the next five years, thanks to a generous grant from Propel.

This is especially timely. The poetry community has paid close and deserved attention to work by minority and female writers and to closing diversity gaps among arts board members, but similar attention has not yet reached to disabled writers. With this series and this effort we hope to begin to remedy that gap.

Our first three poets are Tito Mukhopadhyay, with "Creating the Faces and Other Poems," D.J. Savarese with "Swoon," and our first Propel Poetry Award Winner, Daniel Simpson, with "Inside the Invisible." All three books are stunning, and all are available at our website at $10 each, or all three for $20.

—Bob Herz, Steve Kuusisto, Andrea Scarpino

Nine Mile Magazine

Spring 2023

Vol. 11, No. 1

Appreciations and Asides

Notes on art, literature, and life, gathered here and there from artists and critics whom we love, engage with, and sometimes disagree with.

■ I live between two worlds, the one I see with my eyes open and the one I see with my eyes closed. Unlike other people, I regard the two as equals and trust my eyes as much as I trust my imagination. To favor one over the other is inconceivable to me. Poetry is not just a record of things seen and remembered, but a deeper reading of them with the aid of the imagination. It doesn't take much to get me started: a sock I can't find in the morning, the color of the sky just before it snows, the news on the radio, a pair of broken, expensive-looking wire-rimmed glasses fallen in the gutter, a dog begging on two legs outside a supermarket, the wind sending gust after gust at a woman trying to cross the avenue, causing her to stagger and spin around as it tugs at her skirt like an impatient lover.
—Charles Simic, "The Prisoner of History," The New York Review of Books, August, 2014.

■ William Blake is the British Sade, as Emily Dickinson is the American Sade. Directly inspired by *The Faerie Queene* and its incomplete response in Paradise Lost, Blake makes sex war the first theatrical conflict of English Romanticism. The daemonic wombs of the Gothic novel are too confined for Blake's cosmic drama. In the same decade as Sade, Blake turns sex and psyche into a Darwinian cycle of turbulent natural energies, fleeing, chasing, devouring. The postwar critics who rescued Romantic poetry from low esteem tended to ignore or downplay troublesome sexual and moral ambiguities. For example, Northrop Frye's pioneering study

of Blake, *Fearful Symmetry* (1947), optimistically promotes sexual liberation in a way that seems, a weary generation later, simplistic and naive. How much was hoped from sex. How little sex can deliver. Blake's writing is split by a terrible contradiction: Blake wants to free sex from its social and religious constraints, but he also wants to escape the domination of the Great Mother of chthonian nature. Alas, with every turn toward sex, we run right back into mother nature's dark embrace. Blake's tireless productivity as poet and draughtsman came from the intolerable entrapments male imagination finds itself in when reflecting on nature. Blake's poetry is sexual grand opera of instability, anguish, and resentment.
—Camille Paglia, *Sexual Personae* (Yale University Press, 1990)

■ When you have read *Paterson* you know for the rest of your life what it is like to be a waterfall.
—Randall Jarrell, *No Other Book: Selected Essays* (Harper Perennial; Reprint edition, 2000)

■ Let's assume that someone from an alien world, a Merman, found his way into one of our university libraries and sought to understand us through our literary and scholarly journals. To such a creature, wouldn't the one unifying trait of our criticism (the one linking analyses of Homer to deconstructions of Calvin Klein ads, studies of the theme of Christian recusancy in medieval Icelandic sagas to critiques of subway performance artists) be its elaborate defensiveness? And wouldn't this tell our Merman a great deal about the larger academy where these pieces were bred? He wouldn't have to meet a single critic in order to hypothesize that this is a perilous realm, whose inhabitants perpetually expect to be preyed upon. He could deduce this merely from our penchant

for qualifying our qualifications, for substantiating the inarguable, for running in place while ostentatiously huffing and puffing.
—Brad Leithauser, "'No other book'": Randall Jarrell's criticism," *New Criterion*, April 1999

■ A critic is a man who knows the way but can't drive the car.
—Kenneth Tynan, *The Diaries of Kenneth Tynan,* ed John Lahr (Bloomsbury, 2001)

■ It being hard to make ends meet, the critical ecosystem grows ever more fragile. Many book critics, for instance, rely more and more on chairing events and running literary festivals for income, something that can – and does – take its effect on their reviews. Who is going to be negative about a book by a writer with whom they'll shortly share a green room? Writers do tend to know one another; their air kisses have long graced the literary pages. But the muffled sound of punches being pulled now emanates not only from, say, novelists who occasionally review, but from jobbing writers who make the majority of their income from criticism. Hatchet jobs still get written. These days, however, you're more likely to find a perfectly ordinary book acclaimed as a "masterpiece". Critical inflation is rife, and pity the innocent reader, about to rush out and buy a new hardback.
—Rachel Cooke, "What is the point of a critic if not to tell the truth?", *The Guardian*, March, 2020

…a good poet's made, as well as born…
—Ben Jonson, "To the Memory of My Beloved the Author, Mr. William Shakespeare, and What he Hath Left Us," part of the preface to Shakespeare's First Folio 1623

■ I must confesse that Poets are the whetstones of wit, notwithstanding that wit is dearly bought : where hony and gall are mixed, it will be hard to seuer the one from the other[.] The deceitfull Phisition giueth sweete Syrropes to make his poyson goe downe the smoother: The Iuggler casteth a myst to worke the closer: The *Syrens* song is the Saylers wrack: The Fowlers whistle, the birdes death : The wholesome bayte, the fishes bane: The Harpies haue Virgins faces, and vultures Talentes: *Hyena* speakes like a friend, and deuoures like a Foe: The calmest Seas hide dangerous Rockes: the Woolf iettes in Weathers felles: Many good sentences are spoken by *Danus,* to shadowe his knauery: and written by Poets, as ornaments to beautifye their woorkes, and sette theyr trumperie too sale without suspect.
—Stephen Gosson, *The Schoole of Abuse* (1579)

■ Creativity is: a funny thing. When we're inventing something, we're more vulnerable than we'll ever be. Eating and sleeping mean nothing. We're in "Splendid Isolation," like in the Warren Zevon song; the world of self, Georgia O'Keeffe alone in the desert. To be creative you've got to be unsociable and tight-assed. Not necessarily violent and ugly, just unfriendly and distracted. You're self-sufficient and you stay focused.
—Bob Dylan, "Bob Dylan on Music's Golden Era vs. Streaming: 'Everything's Too Easy,'" *Wall Street Journal,* Dec. 19, 2022

■ ...I think truly, that of all writers under the sun, the poet is the least liar; and though he would, as a poet, can scarcely be a liar. [For] he nothing affirmeth, and therefore never lieth; for, as I take it, to lie is to affirm that to be true which is false: so as the other artists, and especially the historian, affirmeth many things, can, in the cloudy knowledge of mankind, hardly

escape from many lies: but the poet, as I said before, never affirmeth; the poet never maketh any circles about your imagination, to conjure you to believe for true what he writeth: he citeth not authorities of other histories, but even for his entry calleth the sweet Muses to inspire into him a good invention; in troth, not labouring to tell you what is or is not, but what should or should not be. And, therefore, though he recount things not true, yet because he telleth them not for true he lieth not... so think I none so simple would say, that Æsop lied in the tales of his beasts; for who thinketh that Æsop wrote it for actually true, were well worthy to have his name chronicled among the beasts he writeth of. What child is there that cometh to a play, and seeing Thebes written in great letters upon an old door, doth believe that it is Thebes? If then a man can arrive to the child's age, to know that the poet's persons and doings are but pictures what should be, and not stories what have been, they will never give the lie to things not affirmatively, but allegorically and figuratively written; and therefore, as in history, looking for truth, they may go away full fraught with falsehood, so in poesy, looking but for fiction, they shall use the narration but as an imaginative ground-plot of a profitable invention.
—Sir Philip Sidney, *A Defence of Poesie and Poems* (1583)

■ I had thought of the Lycidas as a full-grown beauty-as springing up with all its parts absolute--till, in an evil hour, I was shown the original copy of it, together with the other minor poems of the author, in the library of Trinity, kept like some treasure to be proud of. I wish they had thrown them in the Cam, or sent them after the latter Cantos of Spenser, into the Irish Channel. How it staggered me to see the fine things in their ore! interlined, corrected as if their words were mortal, alterable, displaceable at pleasure! as if they might have been otherwise, and just as good! as if inspiration were made up of

parts, and these fluctuating, successive, indifferent! I will never go into the workshop of any great artist again, , nor desire a sight of his picture, till it is fairly off the easel; no, not if Raphael were to be alive again, and painting another Galatea.
—Charles Lamb, "Oxford in the Vacation," *London Magazine*, 1820. This was a footnote to the essay.

■ …How good/great/important/major is Philip Larkin? Instinctively and not illogically we do bow, in these matters, to the verdict of Judge Time. Larkin died twenty-five years ago, and his reputation (after the wild fluctuation in the mid-1990s, to which we will return) looks increasingly secure. And we also feel, do we not, that originality is at least a symptom of creative worth. Larkin certainly felt so. In a letter of 1974 he quotes a remark by Clive James—"originality is not an ingredient of poetry, it is poetry"—and adds, "I've been feeling that for years." Larkin's originality is palpable. Many poets make us smile; how many poets make us laugh—or, in that curious phrase, "laugh out loud" (as if there's any other way of doing it)? Who else uses an essentially conversational idiom to achieve such a variety of emotional effects? Who else takes us, and takes us so often, from sunlit levity to mellifluous gloom? And let it be emphasized that Larkin is never "depressing." Achieved art is quite incapable of lowering the spirits. If this were not so, each performance of King Lear would end in a Jonestown.
—Martin Amis, "Philip Larkin: His Life and Work," from *The Rub of Time* (Knopf Doubleday Publishing Group, 2017)

■ I had thought of the Lycidas as a full-grown beauty-as springing up with all its parts absolute--till, in an evil hour, I was shown the original copy of it, together with the other minor poems of the author, in the library of Trinity, kept like some treasure to be proud of. I wish they had thrown them in the Cam, or sent them after the latter Cantos of Spenser, into the Irish Channel. How it staggered me to see the fine things in their ore! interlined, corrected as if their words were mortal, alterable, displaceable at pleasure! as if they might have been otherwise, and just as good! as if inspiration were made up of parts, and these fluctuating, successive, indifferent! I will never go into the workshop of any great artist again, , nor desire a sight of his picture, till it is fairly off the easel; no, not if Raphael were to be alive again, and painting another Galatea.

—Charles Lamb, "Oxford in the Vacation," *London Magazine*, 1820. This was a footnote to the essay.

■ In a way my definition of poetry is quite conventional and classical. I believe a poem differs from routine or normal discourse (like this statement,for instance) by being the art form that foregrounds language, in its complexity, intensity, and, especially, *relatedness*. My criterion here is what Aristotle called <u>*to prepon*</u> or fitness. In the poetic text, everything is related to everything else--or should be--the whole being a construct of sameness and difference in pleasing proportions. What makes something "pleasing" can of course not be said outright and depends on the reader, the historical moment, and the cultural milieu. But we can say what poetry isn't: it is not straightforward, expository discourse (as in a chemistry textbook), whose aim is to convey information. I go back to Wittgenstein's proposition (#160) in <u>Zettel</u>, "Do not forget that a poem, even though it is composed in the language of information, is not used in the language-game of giving information.' ... Poetry must meet the criterion of re-readability. If a poem can be absorbed at one reading (as the typical poetry reading demands--i.e., at one hearing), then it's not much of a poem. Poetry is news that

stays news; it is "language charged with meaning" (Ezra Pound). And here Pound's aphorisms accord with Russian Formalism and the notion of defamiliarization, making strange, the orientation toward the neighboring word. But neither Pound's nor the Russian Formalist notion is new: one finds the same formula in Sidney's *Defense of Poetry* or in Johnson's *Preface to Shakespeare*, where we read "Nothing can please many, and please long, but just representations of general nature." I take Johnson's "just" to mean the Aristotelian "fitting" (the *prepon* again), the implication being that representations (whether in lyric, drama, or fiction) must strike us not just as plausible according to some outside norm, but internally consistent and coherent.... "Language charged with meaning" suggests that poetry can never be a matter of "lovely" or "elegant" language but that it must be meaning-ful; on the other hand, "meaning" that is external to or prior to language, as in much of contemporary writing that passes for "poetry" is not poetry either.
—Marjorie Perloff, "Dialogue on Evaluation in Poetry," for *Professions: Conversations on the Future of Literary and Cultural Studies*, ed. Donald Hall (Urbana: University of Illinois Press, 2001

■ Several explanations have been given by various members of the movement as to how it received its name. According to the most widely accepted account, the name was adopted at Hugo Ball's Cabaret (Caf) Voltaire, in Zrich, during one of the meetings held in 1916 by a group of young artists and war resisters that included Jean Arp, Richard Hlsenbeck, Tristan Tzara, Marcel Janco, and Emmy Hennings; when a paper knife inserted into a French-German dictionary pointed to the word *dada* ("hobby horse"), it was seized upon by the group as appropriate for their anti-aesthetic creations and protest

activities, which were engendered by disgust for bourgeois values and despair over World War I.
— "Dada," Britannica, https://www.britannica.com/art/Dada

■ Creeley has become a guru to "language poets"—a term whose equivalent in other arts would be "dancing choreographers' or "music composers" or "food chefs." Literary self-consciousness is as old as poetry itself; every poet is a "language poet." In much of Creeley's work, however, particularly after *For Love*, language itself is the exclusive focus, thereby positing an ideal reader who is a philosopher of language. Wittgenstein would have spent many happy hours with Creeley's poems. My own reactions I can sum up variously, depending on my mood, as: (1) this poetry deliberately avoids communication, for reasons of its own; (2) it is so abstruse that I lose interest; (3) it is simply over my head.
—Richard Tillinghast, *The Nation*, November, 1983.

■ To suggest that a creative writer, in a time of conflict, must split his life into two compartments, may seem defeatist or frivolous: yet in practice I do not see what else he can do. To lock yourself up in an ivory tower is impossible and undesirable. To yield subjectively, not merely to a party machine, but even to a group ideology, is to destroy yourself as a writer. We feel this dilemma to be a painful one, because we see the need of engaging in politics while also seeing what a dirty, degrading business it is. And most of us still have a lingering belief that every choice, even every political choice, is between good and evil, and that if a thing is necessary it is also right. We should, I think, get rid of this belief, which belongs to the nursery. In politics one can never do more than decide which of two evils is the lesser, and there are some situations from which one can only escape by acting like a devil or a lunatic.

—George Orwell, "Writers and Leviathan," *The Complete Works of George Orwell*, Sanage Publishing. Kindle Edition.

Doug Anderson

In Plague Time

At the beginning of our quarantine
I fled my house and drove route 9.
Near Cummington I crested a hill
and saw three vultures at the center line
tearing at a bloody carcass.
Two lifted away, the third stayed.
Above its surgeon's beak, a red-rimmed eye
in its denuded head, held me
as if to say *I know you,*
and returned to its ripping.
Another driver leaned on his horn,
pulled around us with a glare. We left,
the vulture and I. I swung wide
so not to hit the mess and scatter it,
thinking of the vulture's broad-winged circuit,
the shadow of it coming back to feed.

All Over Town

I am aware that at this hour,
in houses and apartments all around me,
people are stepping into their showers.
I make the water hotter as I grow used to it.
Steam rising around me, soothing me,
clearing my nostrils.
I reach for the soap and lather myself,
wash my scant hair, behind my ears,
remembering my grandmother long ago
scrubbing me as if I were a burnt pot.
But I'm gentle now, knowing the hurt places
I've gathered. I tune myself to a lover's hands,
remember the last woman who was good at it.
All over town people are being tender with themselves
in this hour between waking and dressing,
before putting on the gang face to go to work,
chasing away whatever wisps of dreams
might be hanging on. I feel for scars--
above my eyebrows from fighting.
The ridge of my twice broken nose.
The side of my face where they dug out
the big chunk of cancer and the long suture marks
on my neck where they took the graft to plug it.
My throat, a broken cathedral organ of backed up love.
My ailing left shoulder, my once proud chest,
moving on down to the love handles, to the gut
beneath which hide the ribbed muscles.
The fading burns on my hands,
the pitted flesh from the bullet fragments
now mostly covered with tattoo.
My shop-worn cock and my balls hanging all day
in the dark by themselves, scheming.

My disintegrating right knee,
torn ligaments of the other leg,
down toward the feet, almost crushed now
under the weight of a life.
For a moment, at this hour, perhaps we are all
this way. It makes me sad
that we are alone in this holy of holies,
grieving the failing flesh beneath which
Death sits in her carriage loosely holding the reins.

When the Plague Came

and all were shuttered in their houses
the animals came into the cities and filled the streets.
Bears scattered the pigeons, goats raided the grain stores
and vultures stood on the chimney tops and waited.
The King, dying, began to flail with knives
and until they restrained him killed seven courtiers.
The moon was yellow in the iron sky.
When it became full, a madman appeared in the street
at the edge of town, naked and singing.
He was covered with hair and smelled of sileage and dead
    leaves.
The animals gathered around him. A horse bent
to groom him of his lice and a bat hung in his beard.
He said, "salt, wine, blood, gold, and the watering troughs
are full of stars. There is a man under me who walks foot to
    foot
with me upside down, and when he goes left and I go right
the pain makes me love you more than ever, you who have
rejected me as well as those who've left food for me
and crossed yourself in the belief you'll be saved."
He walked on and the animals followed him out of town.
No one knew his name but called him Hornfoot, Root Rot,
Lunato, Cringe and Frederick the Dead.
When the plague was gone and people came out
into the streets to dance, no one remembered him.
He had taken the plague with him.
But they didn't see the wide circle he made through
the fields, then headed back toward them at harvest time.

I Was Preaching to the Choir

and they said I needed
some new material
and I said the old material
is the new material and they said
you need to change something,
different instrumentation
different outfit, something,
and I said you've stopped
singing with me, why?
and they said, it's that organ
and so, I installed new foot pedals
and pull controls that could make it
vibrate all the way through us
into the ground, below theory
below knowledge, on into
something like a soul
where we remembered why
and who we were and how
terrible the world
and we could smell it
taste it hold it against our hearts
and they said, that's better,
now let's start again and I said,
Yes, let's start again,
once more from the top
some songs you can't hear enough.

Mountain Hermitage

Last night I ground my ink,
brought in water and food

to ride out the storm. At dawn,
it's bitter cold, and the rocky path

now too slippery. Even the tigers
are holed up below, the monkeys silent.

I begin to write, stiffly at first,
then the brush slides easily.

How the black words touch life
and bring the color back.

I will sit here until long into the night,
piss out the door,

and go back to work.
Then a candle and a bowl of wine.

It could be worse. I could be
with my wife and lonelier still,

her love faded from me.

Ola Mai

Husband, when we were younger
and became bored

with each other, you wandered
two villages down river

and fucked that girl Phan
behind the temple.

My face was hot. People
snickered behind my back.

Then I went to the harbor
to sell my mats,

and fucked that captain
with the tattooed face.

You scowled for a year,
but now can scarcely remember.

We are old now.
Your knees are bad.

I always help you rise from your bed
but this morning

I need your hand.
I lost my words in a dream,

for a moment forgot who I was.
Is that how it is

when we die and have
not yet found another name?

Felix, Her Parrot

mimicked her having an orgasm.
The men who dated her
had a problem with this.

Moon Leaning

Moon leaning against the backstage wall.
Moon in your pocket.
Moon in the porcelain of the bathtub.
Moon deep in the horse's black eye.
Moon on the backs of my hands.
Moon rising up the spine.
Moon through the roof beams,
grid on the mill floor,
Moon in a fishbowl.
Moon on the woman in the window,
looking out over the street,
cigarette moving back and forth.
Moon in the cat's yellow eye on the green lawn.
Moon on the tip of the tongue.
Moon pulling on something you'd rather stay asleep.
Moon of the insomniacs.
Moon searching for the stream that used to run here.
Moon turning the red maple redder.
Moon in three buckets out by the barn.
Moon on the axe handle.
Moon in a grain of salt.
Moon following me home,
I turn and it's gone,
but there it is in front of me,
one in each window.

Apotheosis

Sade understood
   there was a little of him
      in everybody
and on a moonless night
   caught that priest,
      little girl bent over his knees
         whipping her
            to drive the Devil out,
oh yeah. Sade knew they'd have
      hidden places
         for the hooved half
           of their angel
(dig Lucifer's long star-trail down)
   If there were no dark place
      to hide the stuff, imagine:
everybody walking around
      owning their shit   hallelujah.

Intervals are Cruel

I'll not see someone for a year or two,
then find them on the street, stricken,
moving slowly with a walker.
Not so long ago vibrant,
and full of the future.
It happens so fast.
Or I hear they're in hospice.
A man I remember joyfully married,
now bitter, sitting by himself
in a coffee shop, staring straight ahead.
In a moment we can lose everything.
I pray to go all at once,
doing something I love
then, falling, falling like a tall tree,
softly landing in the fogbound ferns.

We Had a Party Line

The milkman delivered milk in glass bottles.
Our doctor came to the house when we were sick.
We had a TV the size of a toaster
and a wood console radio four feet tall.
I listened to Amos and Andy, the Shadow.
The cars were made out of steel
with no seatbelts.
The movies were in black and white.
When it snowed, we made snow cream
by mixing in milk and sugar.
There was a WPA sidewalk out front.
I was two when World War II ended.
When the Korean War was over
I rode up and down the street on my bike
shouting The War is Over The War is Over.
People looked at me like I was crazy.
That Anderson Kid what now.
I was remembering the boozy celebrations
of my family when WW2 was over;
Didn't people cheer at the end of a war?
After Hospital Corps School at Great Lakes
before I was sent to Camp Lejeune
to learn how to work with marines
I gave my grandmother a shot for pain.
She was dying of cancer.
I was on my way to Vietnam
before the year was over.
I spent 13 months in Vietnam with a marine rifle company.
I came home and the country was falling apart.
Didn't people cheer after a war?
Didn't they ride the returned GIs on their shoulders?
Wasn't there ticker tape?
No. The war was continued inside us for a very long time.

Dear Mr. Auden

Poems slip under the guard
of the self-serious,
wake them in the night
wondering who they are,
and why, after all these years
they are still full of longing. Outside,
the moon turns a wet rose white.
Something, the best of them,
is hiding in the trees. Bid them
step out into the night, open
their robe to the soft uncertainties.
The water heaves its shoulder
into the dam. Here it comes,
brothers, life itself, and no amount
of orthodoxy will save you.
There, Mr. Auden, I can't help thinking
you meant poetry makes everything happen.
Brother, sit up in the afterlife
and drink a shot of vodka to me.
The stars a snail's trail across the black sky.

Facets

A garnet and a diamond are sitting at the bar.
The diamond, looks at himself in the mirror,
so clear about who he thinks he is.
The garnet, a murky red and purple, shrugs.
I've carved my name on glass, says the diamond.
But the garnet's dark heart pulses steady, even.
The diamond sparkles: lights up all the wedding rings
and the husbands turn to look. Someone fondles
the grip of a pistol tucked in his jeans.
The garnet slides off his stool, says his goodbyes,
will happily walk home in the rain,
the music growing fainter all the way.

The emerald does not sit down,
but arranges herself in the chair,
her gown spread just so.
Heads turn. She's looking for the one
but he's not here.
She'll not go home with just anyone.
She orders Drambuie, avoids the diamond's gaze.
Off stage, the stripper
dusts her sweaty thighs with powder.

Carnelian has set his sights on Ruby.
He knows he's not smart
but he knows just what her body needs.
Don't talk about books, he thinks,
you're no match for her.
Ruby's had two drinks, looks at him,
slides off one shoe the toe of the other,
drops it on the floor.

When They Stop Shouting They Can Hear the River

The scholars Thu and Chu fight all the time--
blah Confucius blah Chuang Tzu--
till no one can stand to be around them.
When they grow tired they sit together and feel
the silence fill in the color
of all the black and white they've made.
Birds settle in the trees around them,
hop toward the crumbled leavings of their lunch.
They sit with their backs to the river
where deep down green the big catfish grow.
A girl goes down to the river with a basket of clothes.

Eleven in the Morning at the Monastery

The monk, Tri Hoang, listens to his stomach grumble.
My hunger is an illusion, he tells himself,
but also wonders if they'll have custard
along with gruel when the lunch bell rings.
On his cushion, he sighs, and is then embarrassed.
What if someone heard? He doesn't know
that Minh, the young monk beside him,
is thinking of the village girl, Lan Anh,
who fell in the stream, and when she rose
her breasts could be seen through her shirt.

A Storm is Coming

But the sky's still dazzling blue.
Cat's paws appear on the lake,
but the fields are still bright with sun.
The trees to the north
have just begun to tremble.
Wang Xiu Ying, the magistrate
was once one of us. He dug and plowed
and brought water from the well
but now that he's grown rich
he forgets us. He no longer
takes my hand with warmth,
but gives it a quick squeeze
as if he might catch something from me.
I am rich in ways he does not know.
When I die I'll have a few poems
like peppers picked along the trail.
He'll weep with fear
and fondle his gold in the dark.

This Morning

I saw a golden hawk
above the trees,

and circling within her gyre,
her eyas' smaller one,

their four eyes scanning for
the tiniest trembling in the grass.

I pick up my brush to compose
a short poem.

I've trouble with those,
my hand

has its own ideas about
where the poem should go.

It says, you are not
in control, let be.

And so I've compromised
between short and long.

My hand's now off
to do other things,

piss, put on tea.
Figuring out

is for accountants
and their rattling beads.

Le Sai Meets His Torturer, Ngo Lam

The wheel has turned again.
The old captain of the guard
pares the hooves
of the new lord's horses.
The cook of incomparable feasts
weeds the garden.
Ngo Lam, the torturer,
who's cut his face so no one will know him,
now prunes trees instead of people.
One day Le Sai meets him in the street.
Ngo Lam, he says,
it has been many years and presents his hand--
the one that still has fingers.
Ngo Lam looks both ways and takes it,
his own hand trembling.

Everyone Has Gone to Sleep

And I blow the candle out.
The fragrance from the pines

quickens me.
There is another world here

and because I don't sleep
much anymore

I can tell you the night is alive.
I can see the great overhanging fruit

of the stars, the fields
day-bright from the moon,

reflected in the eyes
of the soft-footed animals

who've come to drink at my spring.
The curtain between life and death

is thin
and when I pass through it

I'll hear nothing but
the soft rattle of the beads.

The Long War

Filthy and bug-bit, I laugh at the memory
of myself on my fine new horse,
and the people who cheered us.
Looking in the pond before I drink
I see a stranger, naked, matted hair.
Then the face of the last man I killed,
tongue twisting in his mouth.
In my mind I try to see my old farm,
but nothing comes to me,
neither rice nor sugar cane.
We have too many miles to go, and mountains.
A monk appears carrying a hot coal
between two sticks, touches the leeches
we have gathered on our legs
from the river crossing. They fall off one by one.

From Dark to Dark

It's cold and colder and I've pulled
a blanket over my shoulders.

I've written seven poems today
and am pleased with one.

I'll go on writing till I nod.
You are far away

and in these uncertain times
I may never see you again.

I'll need another candle soon.
My heart is thick as a bull's. Yes,

I crave you still in spite
of the Buddha's teaching.

Your blue-black hair
and tender mouth, your hands

that so knew what to do with me.
You've taught me much.

My eyes have begun to burn.
I stop and listen to the silence

of the snow and the one dog
that barks from time to time

two villages down river.
Yes, my senses are that live.

We live an instant between
womb and ashes, but what an instant.

ABOUT DOUG ANDERSON

Doug Anderson's book of poems, *The Moon Reflected Fire*, from Alice James Books, won the Kate Tufts Discovery

Award in 1995, and *Blues for Unemployed Secret Police*, from Curbstone Books, a grant from the Academy of American Poets. His play, *Short Timers*, was produced at Theater for the New City in New York City in 1981. His memoir, *Keep Your Head Down, Vietnam, the Sixties and a Journey of Self-Discovery*, was published by W.W. Norton in 2009. His book of poems is *Horse Medicine*, from Barrow Street, was published in 2015. His new book, *Undress, She Said,* was published by Four Way Books in September, 2022. His work has appeared in *The Massachusetts Review, Poetry, Ploughshares, the Virginia Quarterly Review, the Southern Review, Field*, and other publications. He has written critical articles for the *New York Times Book Review, The London Times Literary Supplement*, and the *Boston Globe*. He has received fellowships and awards from the National Endowment for the Arts, the Massachusetts Cultural Council, Poets & Writers, and other funding agencies. He has taught at Emerson and Smith Colleges, the University of Massachusetts, and the MFA programs at Pacific University of Oregon and Bennington College. He is an affiliate of the Joiner Center for the Study of War and its Social Consequences at UMASS Boston.

ABOUT THE POEMS

I wrote these poems during the first year of the pandemic. I had ended a relationship and was miserable, feeling isolated and anxious and had not yet been vaccinated. I went two directions with them: "All Over Town" was internal, from a reckoning with my life, my age, and the inevitability of death. "In Plague Time" was from an actual experience with a vulture while taking a drive to escape my apartment. With "When the Plague Came," I wanted to imagine the plagues of history, perhaps think of myself as a member of Bocaccio's story-telling cohort; *that* was strangely comforting. "Preaching to the Choir" was political, from the feeling that nothing we accomplished in the nineteen sixties remained, or that it was being systematically dismantled; there was no present counterculture, or even a coherent left. I wondered how to speak to this? It would involve self-examination. How might we have a left that was vital and effective but at the same time compassionate, accepting of imperfection, and allowing for humor? What is the left beyond call-out culture? Where is unity?

Interview With Doug Anderson

This interview was conducted by email between Senior Editor Stephen Kuusisto and Doug Anderson in the third week of January, 2023.

SK: Doug, it's a pleasure to be talking with you even if its via email at present. Thanks for taking time to engage with Nine Mile. I'd like to start with something you once said that's always stuck with me. You wrote: "Telling the truth should create its own eloquence, thus, poetry." Right away in "Undress, She Said" you've this remarkable line: "My throat, a broken cathedral organ of backed up love." That's truth and eloquence straight off! I wonder if you might talk a bit about the role of the body in finding truth and eloquence?

DA: Poetry taught me there's no such thing as the Cartesian mind/body binary. This is why I have lit students memorize and recite poetry. The body becomes the instrument whether reading or writing poetry. Poetry is "the word made flesh" if you'll excuse a Biblical reference. I have to confess, I don't know how I write my poems, and when asked to talk about them, I end up working from the outside in. Notwithstanding, you're on to something. The organ is broken, just as all poems are imperfect. When making the invisible visible we are always approximating. I read some anthropology which argues that our knowledge of the world is to a great degree created by language. In fact, language often precedes our experience of it. The more nimble our language, the more of the world we can know. Abstract language, the language of theory, has a blunting effect; poetry reverses that.

SK: To my mind your new book has echoes of Keats's "La Belle Dame sans Merci" in it—that is, there's the imminence of death and the work of the imagination "coming to terms" through the act of writing poetry. Could you talk a little about the difference you've experienced writing poems from the vantage point of aging? These are not a young man's poems…

DA: I've seen two kinds of death. In Vietnam I treated casualties in the field, some of whom were very young. This is death the thief. There was always something perverse about it. I'd tried to keep one of them alive and then came the death rattle in spite of me. It was as if something had reached in from another dimension and snatched them. I carry them in my memory and they will always be there. But the other kind of death comes at the end of a full life; in my case, a long one. There is both the sweetness of life and the suffering. The struggle to make sense of things, to love, to learn to accept mystery without pushing it away with concepts. This is the life I've been fortunate to have, although at times it has not felt fortunate. I survived being shot at to have this life. But it has not been easy. There's been loss and much failed love. I'll be 80 in April and I can no longer rationalize age. I've been one of those "for a man your age, wow," because I've mostly stayed healthy and have good genes. Now I have a cardiologist. Now I have some neuropathy.

In a long life there are always surprises: new insights, experiences. This has been the gift and the curse, e.g.; to watch the country backslide into fascism and cruelty.

I'm thinking right now of Edgar's line in King Lear: ""Men must endure their going hence, even as their coming hither: Ripeness is all."

SK: This question relates to the one above I think. You write about human imperfection in many places, not as a confessional act, but with more irony than the "let it all out" crowd we see today. I'm thinking of the poem "Vulnerable" which has these remarkable closing lines:

> *It is winter now and also, for me*
> *the other winter that has no spring.*
> *Our world has turned dark*
> *and fascists have risen from their graves.*
> *My imperfect life weighs on me.*
> *And this day, in the bitter cold,*
> *I would have at least my breastplate back.*

There's dark, comic irony to wanting that "breastplate back" as if, in dark times, too much vulnerability may be a liability to intelligence. How far off base am I here?

DA: The liability of privilege: much of middle class America has no idea what life is for the rest of the world, or even the unemployed people on the other side of the tracks. They talk about vulnerability as being a new frontier for men, as if they weren't already vulnerable. They talk about "toxic masculinity" as the curse of mankind and imagine a world in which men will become like Mr. Rogers and the world will be pure. I have seen combat hardened men, marines, break down and sob. I've seen working class men broken by the labor they do. The present world is not a nice place; it scares me. I want to protect myself from it. Women have this wish too, only expressed in different semiotics. For the last five years I've been an interview respondent for an anthropologist, Janet Macintosh, who's been writing about the language of the military and has spent a lot of time with combat vets in particular. She reveals how language shapes us. She has a vigorous intelligence and a capacious heart, qualities you don't always find pared in academics. She has been working linguistically on this and will presently have a book. We are much more complicated than the perennial journalistic meta-realities that become fashionable and then fade.

SK: "Tet 1968-2015, A Valentine" is a beautiful poem. It moves from the terrors of war to being among horses. It takes hard work to live with trust after great pain. You manage to put the two experiences side by side, "paratactically" and I wonder if you can talk a little about how this poem came to you?

DA: Again, I have no idea what happens when I write a poem. But here are some facts. For about five years I hung out at a horse rescue, first photographing horses, then being invited into the farm community. There were thirty-two draft horses on the farm: Belgians, Percherons, Shires, and mixes— "Amish horses." At one point I was instrumental in bringing out some vets to be with the horses as part of their PTSD treatment. Draft horses, in spite of their size, are gentle. They are unlike thoroughbreds who'll kick you for fun. They are a paradox of immense power and tenderness. I think the force of war and the recovery from it is in play here unconsciously. Arc light bombing is "shock and awe." You could see the arc of the explosion far away and then the rumble of the explosion seconds later—and the shock wave if you were close enough. My instinct in this poem was, I think, to transform force into gentleness.

Is there a benefit from this as you turned to poetry? I remember Meryl Streep saying: "Acting is not about being someone different. It's finding the similarity in what is apparently different, then finding myself in there."

She's right, of course. Acting is the ultimate act of mimetic empathy. In my case I think acting was the source of my poetry. I memorized thousands of lines of Shakespeare.

Memorizing makes language part of your body. And what language! "Ere from black Hecate's summons the shard-born beetle with its drowsy hums hath rung night's yawning peal, there shall be done a deed of dreadful note." What a blend of the auditory and visual: the drowzzzy hummz of the (deathwatch) beetle pulling the listener into the black maw of night, and ending with four ominous drumbeats. How can that not catalyze an imagination?

SK: Marvin Bell said: "Try to write poems at least one person in the room will hate." I like the line but think in these dark days its love we're after even if its only for one person out there. In "John Ashbery Spoke From a Tree" you write: "To not care is a blessing. Here is my hand." Any thoughts on reaching the one person with the grace of love?

DA: Murial Rukeyser, in her great book *The Life of Poetry,* talks about the fear of poetry. Poetry, like painting, often slips in under one's guard and creates a disturbance. I have seen people angered by poetry because it seems to be stripping away a mask. This is enough to anger someone. Also, we live in a neo-puritanical time when people are obsessed with making language an impenetrable surface of correctness. Much of academic bickering around this comes from projection and self-ignorance.

In short, I don't think you have to try very hard to offend someone these days, and poetic ambiguity is hard for some.

As for love, it is the most threatening of all revelations. "The lunatic, the lover and the poet are of imagination compact." In retrospect, my life has been about love. I grew up in a family that was crippled in love and I had no mentors that might have helped me understand it. It's been my life project to learn about love. It's an inexhaustible subject and it's not only the romantic I'm referring to. It is that without which we are doomed, as individuals and nations.

David Weiss

Like Milk (*after Chekhov*)

When she walks out on her life,
on the remote, sluggish child,
the unworried husband who wears wool socks to bed,
she curses herself: like milk I've turned in a day.

Love's a misfortune that's come
to show her what fortune really is.
What can hold a candle to love,
that insect buzzing your ear all night in the summer dark?

Nor does she know if misfortune
has appeared to thwart or to protect her real desire —
which is the wish, which the despair,
she'd like to know?

Love: a short story come along
to take a long story's place.

A Day in the Country

Maybe God's the old cobbler
   who frees the boy's hand from the knot hole
      he's reached into to steal a cuckoo's egg

for his sister. God, that barefoot,
   old drunkard only his sister can find
      searching the village high and low.

He knows to call the storm holy,
   he knows that rain will end,
      knows which herb stops a bloody nose.

And they tramp the countryside all day,
   the girl exhausted, the boy taking in
      the old man's words:

how a spray of water makes a swarm
   of bees settle, that the sparrow's a pickpocket,
      but a nightingale gladdens the heart.

God's homeless like this old cobbler,
   like this brother and sister. They pass
      the day amid bird-cherry, meadowsweet

and lilies of the valley. A viper
   crosses the lake, its head rippling the water.
      They rest on the bank before going on.

The old man's no god, the children
   are sickly, parentless, yet the boy's
      thoughts are teeming with all

he has seen; he is on fire with what
    he feels as he lies beside his sister
        in a drafty, deserted barn,

no one to tell. When the old man
    returns from the tavern late that night he puts
        bread beneath their sleeping heads. Only

the moon sees this through the planking.
    Only the moon, which doesn't sleep,
        knows who is and who isn't God.

After the Theater

For no reason, a happiness
began to quicken in her breast

That's it. For no reason. Out of the blue.
At first it's a ball in Nadya Zelenina's breast, rolling.
Then it's a wave. Breaking.

It's like first love, at first — the passionate Gorny,
the comical Grondsev; then, it's more like "dear god,
dear god," in the heat of crucifixion.

Unaccountable how incommensurate it is.
And so much! — what to do with it?
A branch is tapping at the window pane.
Go over and open it, Nadya.

Out there is the orchard and the darkness.
Out there, those who love and those who can't.
What better career than to be the dark itself,
and, faintly, beyond the lamplight, stars.

Because This is Chekhov

you feel it keenly:
yearning, and how
incompatible it is
with the yearning of others.
Because this is Chekhov
yearning is never
less than all-
or-nothing, never less
than life-altering.
Just as keenly you
feel its disappointments
which are crushing;
                      this
is why the moment
I love most
in "Verotchka" is when Vera
turns her back on
Ivan Alexeyevich whom
she loves with a desperate
passion she has just
confessed to by the bridge
at the wood's edge
where she has accompanied him
on this final walk —
summer's over,
he's leaving the district
for good, and she's
gone with him along
the road to gain
time and the courage
to bare her soul,
to offer herself

wholeheartedly —
awkwardly at first,
blurting it out,
but having risked it all
and overcome
her fear, she speaks
eloquently,
of the love she's harbored
and the life she wants,
only to discover
that Ivan Alexeyivich
does not love her
in return.
                    Later,
this believer in the new
science of statistics
who has often waxed
soulful and euphoric
under the influence
of her father's liqueurs
will understand that
his is a tepid spirit
able to sympathize with
the vitality and zeal
of others, though incapable
of either himself.
                    Now
in this exultant moment
which she has not let
slip by, he stammers out
his unequal reply.
She straightens up
like a poplar, turns
away and will not

stop for him;
he follows after
entreating her to wait,
though half-heartedly.
He wants mainly
not to be the cause
of her agony.
Yet he will stand
in the moonlight
beneath the unlit
window of her room
before trudging off,
a broken man,
never to see her
again.
       Perhaps
it was dignity Vera fell
back on then;
maybe she was crushed
by the end of all
hope: no escape
from her pinched, provincial
town to those towering
grays of St. Petersburg
where ideas and ardor
struggle to drink
life to the lees,
that romantic illusion.
I prefer to think
she didn't glance back
(although she does once
going in at the gate)
because she's understood
the failure to be his

and refuses to let him
off the hook. No
compromise. Let
living for both of them
never be the same.
Because this is Chekhov,
mere honor and goodness
aren't adequate.
Because this is Chekhov,
there is throughout
the smell of heliotrope,
tobacco plants,
and mignonette,
a common garden
flower, inconspicuous
and fragrant, a figure
for Vera herself.
Because this is Chekhov
the story belongs to
Ivan Alexeyevich
(which is why
Vera Gavrilovna
must remain a mystery):
he is doubly cursed
because he knows
that memories lose
potency with time
(he is all too
poetic on the subject),
and that even this evening
like a figured carpet
shall grow thread-
bare until all that's
left of it's the dust

on his straw summer hat
tossed beneath the bed.
If you turn to the story
you won't find
the figured carpet —
it's mine, as is
the way I'm retelling it.
Because this is Chekhov,
you'll remember the mist
which obscures the near view
but not the stars
as they walk the road,
he lugging his books,
she summoning the nerve;
you'll be struck by the way
the hayricks keep
the mist from dispersing.
Because it's Chekhov
you'll know from that detail alone
what love is for
and you'll know that Ivan
Alexeyevich, right now
packing his trunk
in the small hours,
will never get over it.

David Weiss has published five previous collections of poems: *The Fourth Part of the World* (Ohio State University

Press), *Gnomon* (Wolf at the Door Press), *Perfect Crime* (Nine Mile Books), *Per Diem* (Tiger Bark Press), *Little Mirror* (Lynx House Press), and No One Sleeps Tonight (Tiger Bark Press) and a novel, *The Mensch.* His crime novel series Ditch Witch is available on Amazon. Essays, translations, and poems have appeared over the years in *The Atlantic, Parnassus, The New Yorker, Iowa Review, North American Review, Modern Poetry in Translation, Crazyhorse, Ploughshares* and *Hole in the Head Review*, among others.

ABOUT THE POEMS

These poems in Nine Mile belong to an ms. that retells some short stories of Chekhov in verse. Now, why in god's name would anyone want to do that? Chekhov's stories are already so interlockingly spare and compressed that they already read like poetry. Only an idiot would do a readers' digest version of Chekhov. And it's true, I felt like idiot on a fool's errand. A short story is already the sonnet of fictive prose. In my own defense, I should say that retelling them was more like the experience of picking up a Rubic's Cube. I thought that if I could take a story apart and put it back together without leaving much out, I would understand something about the way a Chekhov story is ordered, and also how Chekhov put together his devilish machines. The aim was to include everything (impossible, of course) and let the telling find its own way to sequence the scenes and details. In this way of thinking about the project, it resembles the oral tradition of story-telling in which a story remains the same and yet is told non-identically each time. Well, that's all true, if not true enough, since every telling told differently amounts to an interpretation.

Part of what I was about was simply the pleasure of telling a story I could never write; part of it was a compensation, also pleasurable, for being narratively challenged — I was writing a novel at the time that involved a good deal of micro-riffing that tried not stray too far into the associative weeds. Channeling Chekhov had to do with that question Yeats' asks in *Leda and the Swan*: "Did she put on his knowledge with his power"? There's all sorts of ways to learn a thing. That was mine. Although the answer to the question about knowledge in my case was no, I didn't. But I did experience a lovely facility. The poem versions fell so naturally into place in the retelling. And for that I felt grateful, especially after the hours of agony and faux-ecstasy of eeking out each day a few hundred words of a scene or part of a scene that hadn't existed before. And when the sun began to slant in the west-facing window of the garage where I worked, I'd turn to Chekhov in order to be enthralled by an effortlessness that did battle against Ananke, that god of necessity who comes to thwart and disappoint. If you read enough Chekhov, you realize that he sides with desire, desire which he knows does not always side with his characters. As one of his stories in my version puts it:

> *you feel it keenly:*
> *yearning, and how*
> *incompatible it is*
> *with the yearning*
> *of others.*
> *Because this is Chekhov*

yearning is never
less than all-or-nothing,
never less than life-
altering. Just as keenly
you feel its disappointments
which are crushing;
　　　　　　this
is why the moment
I love most in "Verotchka"
is when Vera
turns her back on
Ivan Alexeyevich . . . .

And he knew, too, that there are necessities grounded in love and attachment that can marry necessity and desire, a subject Chekhov explores, tragically, for example, in the "Black Monk." Chekhov's urgencies are a poet's urgencies, it seems to me. And maybe that's why I sought out through craft his power in order to understand the panoramic dynamics of his knowledge.

James Cervantes

Commedia dell'arte, an elegy

Hey, wanderer, I do believe I am
losing sanity to time or circumstance.

I laugh like a crow*: racka-racka-racka.*
It means nothing. Why should it?

Come out of your hole, James-A.
Why hast thou forsaken me, Gregorio?

And the Contessa who slammed the door
on my e-mail with poem attached: Why?

Bad bad poem, tail between its legs,
wanting only out of the rain.

Despite its being in thick, crumbly crayon,
this one is for adults with better things to do.

racka-racka-racka, laugh like a crow,
dance like a grackle. O, Illustrated Life!

*

Let's place an order in this disorder.
Humor medium-rare, no running red

insult disguised as job well done.
racka-racka-racka. Turn *la página.*

No need to be bilingual. I'll jump aside
to congratulate you. You knew

it meant *turn the page*; however,
metaphorically, we need an image

to convey that I/we no longer
suffer a plague many times in our heads.

Gone, too, snow-blindness of annihilation,
Doomsday crazynakedfucking, long legs

leading to a spilled cup of gravity. So long
to crocheted versions, the philosophy of

If you can't draw hands, make mittens.
Many new old masters draw blurred feet

that reject rough floors and flutter instead,
embellished with indefinite toes as little wings.

*

After countless leaves, many snows, and many fires,
a blind mole reveals a castle underground. It seems

a vessel at the bottom of a sea, one configured
from the pelvic bones of monsters, instruments

preserved in its bowels, empty still
the hollows of flutes, stringless fingerboards

played somehow by several hands at once,
horns muted by hammered gold; then,

under draperies of dust, a chest stuffed
with costumes tagged *Emperor, King, Prince, President.*

racka-racka-racka. A tablet revived by sunlight
notes that four yards of silk would suit him up,

a measure his dresser named "one curtain."

*

We realize now the fiction of being born to this,
the plywood storefront and two-by-four supports,

distance mimicked by things made smaller and smaller,
less and less remembered. Meanwhile, *Queen of Orchids*

sprouts and multiplies in a tangle that drapes a path,
a guided walk taken by newlyweds disembarked

from ship and plane, from a package purchased
for them so they may stroll among blossoms

scarcely moving, wind no more than breath.
In the animated version, trees sway

and have waists, animals find their voices
and form a choir of warm accompaniment.

Peter and Elsa are interviewed on television
about falling in love during a bombing

and being married in rubble - *racka-racka* -
wherein Elsa recalls anachronistic

clouds of blossoms, and Peter
fifty years later with nose of pollen dust,

jowls flared like soft petals.

*

The children of shipwrecks talk of love
as it was taught to them, happenstance

being a lusterless factor: one family
purchases tickets, another wins them

in a raffle. *It was meant*, they'd say,
like the island that turns on itself.

You can walk paradise for a day or more,
emerge on a sandy spit, and wade across

to the point of your beginning. *It was meant*,
they'd say, like the loss of seasons, like wavelets

that lap the stones of Pireaus and erase
all homecomings. I tell you this as I pat my dog

and my chest fills with belated news
of a friend who has ceased to be,

a weight silent as clouds or fog.
racka-racka, I must make light of this.

"Don't let shadows move toward you,"
I tell him in a dream, but he can't resist

the path right next to him, the one
strung out from endless time, steps into

a whisper of desert beneath one foot
and silence under the other.

*

Thus we account for one by his absence
and go looking for others in a little white town.

Puffs of smoke rise in its theatrical night sky,
trouble brews behind its lacquered doors.

GomezFloresJesus performs seasonal labor
on greeting cards found in the General Store

which enable tourists to lift the little town
between thumb and forefinger and place it

a bit farther down the road. A bookstore
adjoins the hotel where an adolescent

slips from one to the other, working
far too much in both. Either his head slams

down on the front desk, or he collapses
against a bookshelf. There's a buzz

as everything drifts away. A tin can whispers
sick as ten monkeys in a maelstrom, the floor

whispers *I hear a mouse*. It is more
than a door that opens to two

marching bands practicing, flags snapping,
semis downshifting on the steep grade

into town. *racka-racka-racka*

*

He recognizes merchants of the little death
lounging on the periphery of the *mercado*.

Women, astral in *The One Beer Novel*,
are perhaps sometimes caught midway,

slip from flimsy white wraps and slide
out of sandals, nude, though wearing clouds.

How quickly he turns to a yearning
to be inanimate, a segment of pipe

joined at either end to others,
anesthetized, not knowing what runs

through it. And, before someone can warn
"It is happening to us," it has happened

to everyone. The fact is of itself, for itself.

*

The ballerina with pigtails stands wrapped
in a blanket staring at the Pacific

on an Oregon shore. The photo is fifty
years old. Hazy morning light imparts distance

between her and the lens, putting touch
beyond reach. It might have turned that way

between him and her. The cloud that came
to rest on the beach could have dissipated

and left her still as a photograph, nothing
remembered beyond that moment, statuary

forever looking out to sea.

*

Imperative that we open
triangular boxes of magic, lift hats

from the heads of the wide-eyed
who have just sat up. *racka-racka-racka*

Now it's mealtime, then it's showtime,
then time to lie down again. The sun strains

to keep up. Five pointed stars move in unison
when a door somewhere opens and closes,

the black thread from which they hang
discernible against a black void in space.

How can it be? No hands in the mittens,
the house gathering dust, layer upon layer

until there are no edges, no outlines.
Dreams empty into white clouds

against a dark sky, one in front of the other,
flat, as if faking themselves. In them,

pronouns will not find names. We open
eyes to an ache: "Oh, I miss you

so terribly," we say, but the *you*
attaches to no one.

Notes to the Poem

* *Commedia dell'arte* was a performance genre originating in Italy in the 16th century and featured stock characters such as Pantalone, Pulcinella, and Scaramouche. Plot lineswere usually on the themes of sex, jealousy, love, and old age, but evolved to include political satire and the roasting of political figures and regimes.

* *"sick as ten monkeys in a maelstrom"* were some of the last words posted on social media by the poet David Spicer before he died.

* *"I hear a mouse"* were the last words posted on social media by Wendy Battin prior to her death.

* *"The One Beer Novel"* is the title of a poem by the late poet, Jim Heavily, published in his first and only book, The Bringer of Culture (*Hinchas de Poesia Press*, 2018).

ABOUT JAMES CERVANTES

Thanks to the pandemic, in 2020 James Cervantes found himself repatriated in the U.S. after having lived mostly in Mexico for the previous fifteen years. His latest book is *From Mr. Bondo's Unshared Life*, a series of closely related persona poems. *Sleepwalker's Songs: New & Selected Poems*, published in 2012, is comprised of 32 new poems and others selected from six previous collections. He was editor of *Porch* and *The Salt River Review,* and was editor of *In Like Company: The Porch & Salt River Review Anthology* (Mad Hat Press, 2015).

ABOUT THE POEMS

About "*Commedia dell'arte*, an elegy": In the notes to the poem, I give a brief description of Commedia dell'arte, though the poem is Commedia dell'arte in only a very loose way. It is episodic as a Commedia presentation likely was, and involves various characters in common life situations, but any similarity ends there. A "stock character" that gets introduced as a laughing, sardonic crow is my own contribution to the cast of characters. The poem's title classifies it as an elegy because half way through the writing I realized I was dealing with a series of losses and goodbyes and their larger meanings. Sadly, a number of those were the deaths of poets who were close friends.

LaWanda Walters

Elegy for Kate Spade

You made a purse significant,
an art that could contain
bobby pins, tissue, lipstick—
all our little vain supplies.

Your art just barely could contain
how bad things felt, the zipper's pinch
at who we are, our vain supplies
for staying happy in the universe.

It was a shock, how bad you felt,
you whose advice was to live "colorfully,"
staying happy in the universe,
the practical purse that fit any occasion.

You, whose advice was to live "colorfully,"
remind me of my best friend in Junior High.
A purse designed to fit whatever occasion—
she was pretty and kind, able to fit in.

You remind me of my friend—
how neat she was and optimistic,
so pretty but kind, too, prepared for class,
her compact body in a pencil skirt.

She kept herself so neat and optimistic,
her drive to be good, hair perfect, flipped up—
her compact body in a pencil skirt
which she could not see in a mirror.

Her drive to always look and be good
was dangerous. Why did she try so hard?
She could not see in the mirror
how cute she looked in a bathing suit.

I might know why she tried so hard.
I heard her younger brother call her fat.
She looked so cute in a bathing suit!
"I think I'm just pleasantly plump,"

she said, that day he called her fat.
She really must have believed him,
although she replied, "I think I'm pleasantly plump."
Her brother was in that stage, disliking girls.

Nevertheless, it was him she believed.
She confided in me, wondering if this could be bad—
her brother had asked if she would put her mouth
on his thing if he wore a sock on it.

She wondered, and I didn't know if it was bad.
To us both, it just seemed weird.
Her brother asked if he wore a sock on it—
and no, none of us knew it might be bad.

Animal Husbandry

He worked in the Department of Animal Husbandry
at State and kept some hogs for his own use,
out on their land, half-an-hour's drive from where he taught
as a professor. He was a handsome man, had six kids,
including my first husband. I got a close-up view
of how a man learns from his dad to beat

a woman up. At five years old, Jack saw his dad beat
his mother, throw her against the stove. "Husbandry"—
isn't that a terrible word? We can view
the word "husband" in this definition of the "use"
of animals, "husbanding" them to slaughter, like goat kids,
cows, pigs. That's not fair, either. But his father taught

this, and he was the head of the department. Jack saw his taut-
muscled, blue-eyed dad, a university professor, haul off and
    beat
his mommy up. She lost teeth, there in front of the kids.
I wonder how close this came to her husband's
murdering her? So is this an interesting variation on the use
of animal husbandry? There are studies that suggest the view

that domestic violence is a cycle—after the wedding vows
the son imitates his father. Those things are taught
even if the son hates the dad, refuses
that knowledge. In my twenties, my husband beat
me too. I got away, threw my wedding band
out into a field. His mother had those kids

in the fifties when mothers got beaten in front of their kids
and kept having babies, going to church. I had a different view
because of the times, when abortion wasn't banned.

Their family, pretty as the Waltons on TV, taught
me how things go. He'd cry after he beat
me up, and I thought that was love. You get used

to it and try not to make them mad, or refuse
them or get into an argument. And I didn't have his kids.
You'll **never** *get away if you have this baby.* Seeing I'd been
    beaten
up, one friend said, "I think of how you'll be in ten years."
    That view
of what would happen saved my life. The father must have
    taught
more sons the lesson. The wife of one used a crowbar on her
    husband

when he was passed out from Coors Light. Animal Husbandry
means the use of another being. In court, their kid said how her
    dad beat
her dachshund puppies. It is hard to view what some are
    taught.

Salman Rushdie Has Been Stabbed

I remember that amphitheater, even if it's been
rebuilt: the stage where my sister played
the Prokofiev Second Piano Concerto
with the Chautauqua Symphony. She'd won
the contest and so I went there and stayed
all summer, stealing the cookies the lady
whose rooms I was cleaning left on her bureau—
an invitation I tried to resist. At the end
of the summer, she gave me a twenty-dollar
bill in a sweet card. Being a chambermaid
there in the summer was a delight—I chose
to sleep in the linen closet because it was
deliciously dark and the smell of old houses
in the morning was of mothballs and cool
air in spite of all the sunlight. One morning
we were hysterical, ducking the bats we'd surprised
in one room. My sister's boyfriend asked me out
and his kiss was disappointing. And my sister
played the concerto. There was blood
on the keyboard from her knuckles
as she bowed to the crowd—the same stage—
and on another day I got to sit in that audience
and hear John Ciardi, and now this other
morning, Salman Rushdie has been stabbed,
and my sister said she wasn't nervous because
she was thinking of me there in the second row.
There was a tape of the performance
that our father managed to lose somewhere.

Children at Twenty

Daughters still cuddle, back home in the mornings.
Sons are more like werewolves, in between
late afternoon and the shaved glaze of high noon,
gawky and uneasy, trigger-happy, gorgeous with acne
and wild outcroppings of hair here and there.
Manhood has surprised them
and they have that sleepy, gruff tone,
not sure how kind to be to their mothers
to be kind. And so I stroke his face, my son's,
and he puts up with it, given he is home for a day more
before riding the bus back up to Chicago.
He is mad at me because I can't smile right
for his camera-phone. I am the one
who is self-conscious, now,
entering the adolescence of old.

But he lets me kiss him, which I know is generous,
and my cheek feels his—bristly in places, silky in others.
It is awkward for everyone, this sadness,
the pressure he has put on himself,
taking math from the professor whom everyone calls the
    pirate,
an eye patch and peg legs from diabetes,
who fell one Saturday, teaching some honors kids
in the seventh grade. "And guess
who helped me? No one!"
He told my son's class the story
of the table he was sitting on
crashing down, no one moving but him
as he took his aluminum legs off, swung himself,
strong as an ape, up onto a chair,
reattached the legs. "Have you ever

seen anything like this?" he asked one twelve-year-old.
"Noooooooooo," she said.

We're close-knit, the three of us, but unravelling,
of course, with time. Our paths will curve
so far apart, one day, I won't see
where either of my children is. I think about such pressures—
the physics, the math, and some girl he might like.
My daughter's bravery, observing a neurosurgery.
Upset, she'll make herself practice the clarinet.
She has switched, in senior year, from pre-med to comp lit,
reading Mishima in Japanese.

At some heart-rending moment, in the car from Chicago,
her mother and brother said "Shut up, Tess."
She had tried to straddle
some argument, pulled hard at the reins—
our charioteer, too understanding of the sun's rounds.

Love's Error

Love gets in a painter's eye like sun,
like a surgeon gets in his own way
if the patient is his wife or little son.
Sometimes the sun's error is what you see

in a photograph—not a blur, just noon's
blue dazzle between the mother's gaze
and the object of her affection,
the baby girl with red hair like hers.

Dazzling, how much we can love a child
or parent. In the photograph with my dad
a kind of white space or caesura, odd as a time lapse,
haloes our conversation on the steps—

my dad and I smile in a haze of noon and shade.
I see, now, what the camera caught was love then.
I am five, we are sitting on the steps, smiling,
and my mother must have taken the picture,

the camera-caught space that makes me swallow
and remember that once we were friends.
My mother must have taken the photo,
my little sister climbing on his shoulder,

and I can remember that once we were friends.
Everything was level, he'd say "When I was a little girl,"
and my little sister was climbing on his shoulder
so many years before the arguments, his glare at me.

He'd brush my teeth and say "When I was a little girl,"
as if there were no barriers between our souls, ever,

so many years before the arguments, his glare
when he disapproved of certain books that I read.

Once there were no barriers between us, ever.
Then Mama bought me the two-piece, or maybe his affair
dirtied his mind, or the books I was reading shocked him
so he saw me like my mother, that grown-up girl.

When Mama had me model the swimsuit, he mourned
that I was "growing up." Then his affair with a girl
in the junior choir came out, and Mama called her terrible
    names.
When I tried to protect her that night, he swung me around

because I had seen him with the girl in the choir
when Mama and my sister were away at music school.
He swung me around by the brush rollers in my hair
when I tried to protect my mother.

Mama and my sister were away and I saw them
on the bed, lying as still as two statues, acting nonchalant
when I tried to protect myself from realizing
it was odd, even with clothes on, to lie on a bed

acting nonchalant when I walked in, like it was normal,
their bodies as still as the stone legs in "Ozymandias."
I tried to believe their Sunday nap
but their bodies were like that poem we'd read in school.

They were lying still, like two sunbathers at Gulf Shores,
and I tried to believe that adults took naps sometimes,
their bodies like the poem we had studied in school,
as still as statues, as nonchalant as sunbathers.

Mama found out they were on her bed.
I had tried not to see too much, and they
acted like it was nothing, like lying out in the sun
and sunlight is necessary but sometimes too much,

his seeing me the wrong way, grown up like the girl
he'd had an affair with. It was as if we saw each other
too well, and hated what we saw.
Never again that blur of love, that parasol.

Before the Formal Feeling Comes

sometimes there is a stopgap—a pain blocker
or some kindness from a doctor who delivers relief,
prescribing oxycodone, instead of being afraid of getting

heat because of the well-reported "opioid crisis"—
like the doctor in St. Simon's Island
who suddenly cut my mother off, off, off
the medicine he had given her for years,

so that suddenly she was back in pain more
ferocious than before, jolted back into
a movie theatre where the Tingler steps out
of the film with his buddy, the Joker,

for a smoke, and then he sees her and points
his pincers at her—this was before people carried guns
to the movies and started to shoot the audience—
and begins to pinch, like Paganini playing pizzicato,

the nerves in her back, transforming the piano teacher
into her grand piano, sending her into spasms
she tried not to voice, but we knew the tone
when her pain was deepest—the *oh* or *uh* or *ooh*

as someone tried to move her—well, the last five years
of her life were a jail cell made of pain—
which pain I carry, having inherited it,
pain like a long whole note that stays,

except I have just been treated more
courageously by a doctor in the ER—
not the handsome one with beer on his breath

who asked me if I had a "chronic prescription"

but some other physician's assistant who saw my pain,
had mercy. Christianity surely was born and borne
on those stories of pain relief. Now some think it means
being careful only of themselves. And hurt us all.

ABOUT LAWANDA WALTERS

LaWanda Walters is the author of *Light Is the Odalisque* (Press 53, Silver Concho Poetry Series, 2016). Her poems have appeared in *Poetry, Georgia Review, Antioch Review, Ploughshares, Cincinnati Review, Shenandoah, The American Journal of Poetry, Live Encounters Poetry & Writing*, and other literary magazines, as well as in *Best American Poetry 2015* and

Obsession: Sestinas in the Twenty-First Century. She received an Ohio Arts Council Individual Excellence Award in 2020. She lives in Cincinnati with her husband, poet John Philip Drury, in a hundred-year-old house on the edge of a wooded ravine.

ABOUT THE POEMS

In my poems, I find myself compelled to write about stories (mine and others'), hoping that in the process of composition I can, while confronting a difficult circumstance, make sense of it—hoping to find a bit of blue sky. I often work with forms, taking liberties as I proceed, to help find that bit of daylight, that song, that buzz, without cheating or being sentimental.

"Elegy for Kate Spade," for example, is a pantoum whose focus on the late designer shifts to recollections of a childhood friend and her brother. "Animal Husbandry" moves within the labyrinth of a sestina to explore incidents of my abusive first husband's violent family. "Salman Rushdie Has Been Stabbed" follows the precedent of Frank O'Hara's "Lana Turner has collapsed" to consider the connection Chautauqua now has not only for the wounded Mr. Rushdie but also for my piano-prodigy sister, Susan Walters (now a performing pianist with the New York City Ballet), and myself (then a chambermaid in the Institution's hotel).

The other three poems talk about the complexities and nuances of family experiences and interactions. One of them, "Love's Error," also uses the leap-frogging repetitions of the pantoum in a casual way, often repeating just a word or a phrase instead of a whole line, sometimes skipping the repetition entirely, letting the form come and go, ebb and flow, celebrating love and lamenting errors, "that blur of love, that parasol." In consorting with forms, I'm not a strict constructionist.

All six of these poems are part of a book manuscript I recently finished and have begun circulating. It's called *Seedy Lake*, a play on T. Coraghessan Boyle's short story, "Greasy Lake."

John Philip Drury

You Are Like Sunrise (*after Hafez*)

(Hafez, ca. 1315-1390)

You are like sunrise. I'm the candle beside a bed.
When you smile, my love, see what my light's forfeited.

The stain of love, dark as your hair, imbues my heart so much
that when I die, my tomb will host the violets' flowerbed.

Waiting at the entry of what I desire, I open my eyes:
you cast your whole self towards me with a glance of your
    head.

O rabble of griefs! How can I thank you? God preserve you.
On the day I'm deserted, you alone will stand in my stead.

I'm enslaved to my pupil, who, despite his black heart,
rains a thousand teardrops when I tell how my heart has bled.

The rising sun radiates across the sky like an idol
but no one worships as I do, gazing overhead.

If my love, like a fragrant wind, glides by the tomb of Hafez,
passion will tear my shroud into pieces, though I'm dead.

In the Light Air (Dans l'air léger, dans l'azur rose) (*after Leconte de Lisle*)

(Leconte de Lisle, 1818-1894)

In the light air, before the sun,
A gold thread shines, thin as a sliver,
On gloom that's watered by the dawn.

Winged flower that blooms when day's begun,
The bird awakens, flies from cover
In the light air, before the sun.

Your soul, O rose, the bee drinks down!
The tamarinds—full, rustling—waver
On gloom that's watered by the dawn.

Mist that stirs when a breeze comes on
Will open into bloom and hover
In the light air, before the sun.

And the ocean, where the skies recline,
Rolls its imposing, sweet palaver
On gloom that's watered by the dawn.

But eyes I've loved and thought divine
Have closed, and that will last forever
In the light air, before the sun!

ABOUT JOHN PHILIP DRURY

John Philip Drury is the author of five books of poetry: *The Disappearing Town* and *Burning the Aspern Papers* (both from Miami University Press), *The Refugee Camp* (Turning Point Books), *Sea Level Rising* (Able Muse Press), and *The Teller's Cage* (forthcoming from Able Muse Press in Fall 2023). He has also written *Creating Poetry* and *The Poetry Dictionary*, both from Writer's Digest Books. After 37 years of teaching at the University of Cincinnati, he's now an emeritus professor of English.

ABOUT THE POEMS

In 1994, when I was putting together *The Poetry Dictionary* for Story Press, one of my goals was to include examples of various terms, and for traditional poetic forms I sought out model poems that displayed each poem's techniques, even in translations. In some cases, I couldn't find satisfactory examples, so I decided to translate them myself. That was easy when I knew the language well enough to work with originals, as I did in translating Jean Passerat's prototype for the villanelle from the French, but it was problematic when I didn't know a language at all and had to find prose versions or verse translations that didn't incorporate the meter and rhyme.

I was also interested in poems that successfully altered or corrupted the rules for a form, and that led me to Leconte de Lisle, who wrote a 13-line villanelle (omitting the usual fourth and fifth tercets) that begins "Le Temps, l'Étendue et le Nombre." When I recently took a fresh look at my extra translations not used in the dictionary and began fiddling with the phrasing, I still wasn't happy with my version of that one, but I liked my translation of another villanelle of his, "*Dans l'air léger*," in which he omits the expected 19th line (repeating the second refrain). I hear that absence as a resonance of loss, an omission that's poignantly expressive. I've imitated the original's octosyllabic meter by resorting to iambic tetrameter, and I've followed the usual rhyme scheme, even though Leconte de Lisle departs from it in the first two lines of the final stanza, where he switches from the A and B rhymes of "*-ose*" and "*-uit*" and introduces a *rime riche* couplet that I couldn't duplicate or approximate in English: "*j'aimais*" ("I loved") and "*jamais*" ("never"). I did use "I've loved" within that first line and "forever" (the reverse of "*jamais*") as the rhyme word in the other.

I had written about ghazals in a previous book, *Creating Poetry*, but I didn't know the traditional rules until I read John Hollander's brilliant verse explanation of the form in *Rhyme's Reason*. (This was before Agha Shahid Ali had begun to champion the traditional form and publicize the rules.) I found a book, *Hafez: Dance of Life* (Mage Publishers, 1988), that included contemporary verse translations, prose translations, and both transliterations and calligraphy of the Persian originals. I didn't like the verse translations, but the nineteenth-century prose versions by Lieutenant-Colonel H. Wilberforce Clarke, taken from *The Divan, Written in the Fourteenth Century, by Kwāja Shamsu-d-Dīn Muhammad-i-Hāfiz-i-Shīrāzī* (1891), proved invaluable. The ghazal I translated and put in the dictionary uses both the *qafia* (monorhyme) and *radif* (refrain) of the form, but many of Hafez's ghazals use just the rhymes, and "You Are Like Sunrise," which I versified and freely adapted from Volume II of the *Divan* (Poem 378, page 652), appears to be one of them. The transliterated rhymes of the original are *sahar-am* and *separ-am* (both in the opening couplet), *dar-gozaram, az-nazar-am, ze-sar-am, semar-am, negar-am*, and *be-dar-am*.

It's possible that the suffix "-*am*" is a refrain after the rhyme of "*ar*," but I don't think so.

In the Winter-Spring 2004 issue of *New England Review*, Dick Davis, virtuoso formalist poet and Professor of Persian at the Ohio State University, declared in an essay titled "On Not Translating Hafez" that the 14th century ghazal master was "held to be untranslatable." But in 2012 Mage Publishers (followed by Penguin Books in 2013) issued his amazing *Hafez: Faces of Love*, which contains his translations of 72 ghazals by Hafez—not including the one I've translated here.

Allen Guy Wilcox

Winter Radio

Whatever it is I'm listening to
on the radio is lovely—coming through
dad's old *Realistic* wooden cabs and
Cheshire amp with an old spin-dial tuner
that lets me jog through stations like Hans Arp, or was it Jean,
playing with paint, composing according to the laws of
    chance.

No vocals on this one—so let me try and piece it together:
Two violins doubling a melody. A Romantic swell, but this
    can't be Brahms.
The doubling gives the tune a slightly eastern feel—it's
    wedged in and drowsy,
as I would have been, in a Bills Starter jacket in the back of
    my dad's truck.

You're listening to WCNY, Classic FM, 91.3 in Syracuse,
89.5 in Utica, 90.9 in Watertown. The man with untold years
    of Catholic magisterium
in his voice would pause then heartily, and speak his next
    words slowly, like divine augury.

That was the Syracuse Symphony Orchestra, performing
    Mozart's Requiem Mass in D minor,
Köchel-Verzeichnis, K. 626, conducted by Musical Director,
    Kazuyoshi Akiyama.

Could I have invented this? *My Old Kentucky Home* with
    horns and kettle drum? The composer is playing with my

expectations, now. Variations on the old songbook—myself
   now a dad,
the title having passed to me at the top of the pandemic—
Orange Blossom Special
with panflutes and tubular bells? Now, it's the conductor
   who's letting off
smokebombs and running interference for the cellos and
   French horns, the sarcastic oboe,
who scatters mustardseed across our driveway
in lieu of the typical magnesium chloride, or Will's quick
   handfuls of tablesalt,
thrown over the shoulder for luck.

Like advent season, this music is designed to build towards a
   climax,
even if I'm going to have to defer the payoff. Sexed-up clarinet
reenters the fray—a bachelor for life—every trick from
   Gershwin searing like a glove warmer
in the front pocket of his black jeans—long-legged like a
Fantastico from an old play.
My time on the sofa tonight asks me to rethink my old
   dreams—kid and wife asleep in bed.
I can feel something pulling me to the back porch,
away from the fire and the sofa, away from my wife and my
   daughter—
back out there into the purple and black ravine, upsetting deer
   stalls as I claw my way through black branch and bramble
to that spot I still hold sacred in my mind, the break in the
   canopy where snow falls into the cold water of Palmer's
   Creek, shifting quietly in hand, like one of dad's unfinished
   Martinis, beneath a layer of cracked ice.

You're in Luck

Lovers neck behind the henge,
Serpents dance along the deck.
Remember that thing you ordered?
Actually, can I see you for a sec?

Naples naps along the shore,
Monsters brush their teeth with trees.
The bathers hum in sacred ponds,
"She thinks I have no eye for these."

That thing you wanted? Got it for you.
Eat a peach right off the truck.
That thing you asked for?
You're in luck.

The Red Goose

It was a morning when breaking the seal of the garage door
and turning to look over the frosted yard, tears came to my
   eyes: it was the cold,
untreated wood starting to crack in the greenhouse.

When there she stood,
her noggin sprung like an old lighter, the red goose,
Traipsing and then sputtering in the frosted green-gold yard.

My daughter yelling at me from the window to *go away*
and her mother saying she's tired, she's tired is all—
go away daddy.

Already I'm in another world,
the snow lifting off the polycarb like an old starlet
in a new picture, the whimsical granny click-heels.

Whereas for daddy, certain complaints only are registered,
   even
intoned. So if the pint-getting, spare-hour boys are pulled
   away by wives and late work,
there's a lot of whistling—*the poor goose darted—*

into the corners of the mind,
mind constructed anyway of two by fours,
twenty four inches on the center,

since we economize where we can.

The Snowy Cow Hills at Suppertime

Away in a manger, no crib for a bed.-Anon.

What's inevitable ain't precisely
the same as what's good,
lasting, or natural. Fresh snow
rips through the cedar canyon
as in a halftime Coors commercial, a tipsy
spray of golden sun the clearest image God could find for
    hope, besides...
The red-haired snowboarder,
launched from the glistening white ramparts
of a man-made Mt. Olympus, in Parking Lot C of the Mall of
    America.
Fans wave their tricolor kerchiefs along the artificial palisade
    cliffs, raising precision-cut wine flutes, and exposing for an
    instant their unctuous pink lips from behind fresh N-95
    masks, as the Taittinger comes, as it often does,
gallantly streaming.

The question appeared to resolve itself and no wonder...

You can see Sagittarius rise in the East, that deft archer, past
    the leftover barrels
of latke-foils and platters of applesauce,
through the pop-up stands
of palm fronds in a vase, and past a parade of healthy
    Breadhouse donkeys who'll lower their necks like a
    Targaryan dragon, if you say the magic word.

Look where he's aiming.

I just want to be home—away from this endless

Mall—back to my people, back to
the crescent ridgeline all white and blue and black,
where one could believe even God patiently side-strokes
each evening through the watery tides of heaven.

I'll stand at my back deck, lullaby-laden and
ripping through the *ostinato* section of my star-chart with
    raging mallets worn,
on a borrowed high school timpani, imbuing a new cadence of
    sharp tonalities with an inner, celestial whale song.

How natural it all is now, or inevitable?

Tonight, in the mirrored glass of the ice
storm I'll fine-tune the next precise
wrong move in my portfolio, catching a glimpse of my late,
    great Great Auntie, that wiley old broad, no longer old—
    catch her crushing a Coors can under the imperious heel
of her fur-lined snowboot, the way she'd done it since high
    school, and her first local banking job. And catch her
    climbing into her Camarro, hauling ass again, skyward.

A friendly *beep beep* from an old Chevy climbs
in counterpoint, through
the snowy cow hills at suppertime
bringing a letter for Santa, half a roast,
and a fresh sixer. Muffler *put-puts* like a cartoon tractor.
Aunt Betty's red Christmas mugs from West Germany that my
    father
picked up at Reid & Sheldon's in '81,
those have been returned to us now, chipless.

In perfect yuletide condition.

All year it's been stuck, my consciousness, or,
put it to you like this, my window has to be cranked a bit
    harder is all,
to get a cross-breeze going.

There is only one story—and, hell's bells, it's death
And rebirth—grafted like skin taken from the shin.

You were caroling now, but this just in: you're all right
about practically everything, given every given.
All is forgiven. Drinks are on the house.

But listen—and this is something I tell
to all first-time winners—if you don't want it, don't stress over
    it.
Promise me you understand
one thing about this place—the valleys,
the malls, the snow-covered gorge, the places we congregated
    when we were young,
might as well say it to you now, and I know
you've heard it before, old pal.

If you don't want it, you don't have to have it.

ABOUT ALLEN WILCOX

Allen Guy Wilcox was born in Cooperstown, NY, and raised on his family's farm, Woodshill Homestead, in Sauquoit. He graduated from Middlebury College in Vermont with a degree in English literature and minor in Religion, and lived and worked for fifteen years in NYC before returning to the farm, where he now lives with his wife and daughter. In 2016, Allen helped found The Theater at Woodshill, a 501(c)3 non-profit Shakespeare theater company, where he serves as Artistic Director. On the stage at  Woodshill he has performed the roles of Benedick, Orlando, Hamlet, Oberon, and Theseus, and he made his directorial debut in 2022 with a production of *A Midsummer Night's Dream.* Allen is also the founder of Time's Arrow, a new way for students to explore literature online in a highly contextualized, multimedia-supported environment. More at woodshill.org & timesarrow.org.

ABOUT THE POEMS

What I know for sure is that I write poems when my daughter goes to sleep, usually on the sofa with my legs crossed, or in an armchair. I write poems on yellow legal pads, usually set onto a clipboard, using inky black or colored pens. I know for sure that I become attracted to what I'm working on when my voice feels warm, inviting, and free to ask questions. This is true no matter what the subject of the poem might be. For me, writing poetry—not unlike reading—is a practice that allows me the opportunity to sift through a jumble of thoughts and impressions, and see if I don't turn up with an aesthetic connection between a few seemingly fractious elements. I rarely arrive with a plan. It's best when that point of connection arrives as an insight, or at least if it allows me the chance to properly pay my respects to this our life, exempt from public haunt, merely by kissing the hem of its radiant garment. In that sense, composing a poem feels to me like delivering a performance; I know that what I can give over to it is—like all things I care best about in life, I guess—simply my undivided attention.

Martin Willitts Jr

Harvesting Corn

I brush-swim-walk through fields of corn stalks.
I must be careful: it is easy to get lost
in the greenness. One assumes all I need to do
is return straight back the same way I entered —
only entering a corn field doesn't work that way.

I am six, among the tenitive brush of corn silks
and green leaves, blindsided by terror-loss.
I settle my heartbeat, stand still, collect my senses,
focus beyond the deception of distance,
listen to the outside world beckon me back.

The greenness tries to disorient me.
Corn tries to swallow me with deafening voices
inviting me to stay forever. Such soothing voices
tell me to leave behind everything I know.

It would be so easy to never return.
I've seen old people do it, tossing away their breath
into the universe.

It would be so easy
to remain in the green labyrinth, ignoring
my grandfather searching for me with lantern light,
ignoring grandmother's supper of potatoes, chicken,
and lima beans.

I need to un-think my way back. Whole whorls of corn shift
side to side like a passenger train. The corn tries hypnosis.

I am here to check on the process of early corn.
Now, I must become one with the plants, see far
out of the clutches of the illusion greenness creates.

No two corn fields or wild, untrimmed forests are the same.
Think of the greenness peeling my mind,
like leaves uncovering corn,
the wind teasing me with brown, silken, corn fibers.

Why Love Does Not Need Restrictions

In the apple-blossom-bite air,
the horses are loose in the back acres, exploring spring.
It's no surprise their hearts are melting,
finding an extra kick and buck.
The horses smell the world
and its endless possibilities tempt them.

The world contains smears of clover,
and the wildness has no reins. This is when
their legs release, stroll, graze.
This is when I brush your hair like a horse's mane,
each strand holding flecks of springtime daffodil-light.

Whatever pleasures we are given in life can be taken away
or can roam free without fences. It is up to us
to encourage love so we do not need white fences.

I stack love
like I stack, pitchfork loose hay
in anticipation of lasting
throughout cold, long winter snows.

Memory also works this way: once contained,
it pitches eventually away.

Survival of the barn animals depends upon our guesswork,
our preparations, our distributing love over time.
The horses keep intense watch.
And, isn't this love, how we gauge reactions?
It's no surprise we try to make love last.

It's no surprise we try to keep warm in winter,

those long-suffering days.
I keep pitching hay and love.
I must make every ounce last. I can't guess wrong.
I've been fooled by spring
when another snow-burst ruins my plans.

After leaving the barn, I return to you and the familiar,
to settle down without the need for fences.
I brush your hair as you lean into love,
the easing of clover appearing in spring.

Math Savant

Incredible — I can "see" equations in my head.
I'm not certain if they've invented the right words for me.
As a child, I stood out, scribbling in notebooks
the four exponentials conjecture on the transcendence
of at least one of four exponential combinations of irrationals.
By now, you are asking, what did he say? I say answers
float in front of me like colors or musical notations.

For years, I could not find the right diagnosis
in the *Diagnostic and Statistical Manual of Mental Disorders*.
Finally, I find a category for me —
apparently, the ability to see numbers as colors is Synesthesia,
and as music is Chromaesthesia.

In fourth grade, I wrote trigonometry
seeing blue quarter notes in the key of A seventh.
The teacher slapped my hand. She wanted me to focus
on fractions, so I calculated the exact number of students
who would fail the exam. I could explain Brownian Motion
as the random motion of particles suspended in gas.

I drew periodic tables in sixth grade,
wanting to play with chemicals with a mad scientist gleam.
I already understood torque and lift off calculations
before the first rocket went into space. Numbers bored me.

In the Principal's Office, I was instructed to stop
embarrassing the teachers, to normalize, to pretend
numbers were not in a conga line dancing.
They wanted me to "break the solution down,"
but answers were yellow, flashing by my head.
I knew Fermat's Last Theorem

contains a length of 5,320 letters. I can't explain
my unexplainable process;
answers just appear in my head.

The Filly

a filly shudders and flickers
in the blossom of spring
she snorts in
the touch of honey buzzing in the air

I sing to her

the filly disassembles in bright
penetrating light and illusion
blending with the backdrop of copper tree trunks

I sing about fresh clover and no fences

her tail swishes spring-light
I toss away the saddle
refusing to break her spirit

I sing love as vast as an endless field
with the tree-blur

I am rewarded when the filly nears
following my song
sniffing my carrot greens

she nudges untying love
her brown eyes relinquish doubt
her flanks ease

I do not have to tame this horse

the filly leans into my love
like a woman snuggles

because no lover should be forced into love

I am nose to nostril
as the filly whinnies like a cooing woman

the world shimmers
flickers
sighs
as love blossoms in early spring

I Start Before the Sun Wakes Up

Before first light, before the sun even thinks of rising
out of its bed from under its star-blanket,
before birds rev their engines, before leaf rustle,
I am in the barn milking cows by hand,
tugging slightly their nipples,
coaxing squirts of milk
like fits of rain, into a metal pail, splashes
of jubilee and release —
that sweet milk-making musical sound
like an ease-down-all-day dripping-rain
quiet as a barn cat licking its paw from milk-spill,

you know,
that same satisfied look people broadcast on their faces
after making thrashing-love —

until the spilling-sound ringing on metal edges quiets
as fresh milk fills to the top.
I pour the milk into a large, white container for market.

I let cows clang bells, heading out to pasture.

With the cows' urges spent, I mosey-on over
to the chicken coop, lift each layer,
caress some eggs into a different metal pail,
leave some eggs to hatch.

If some cows or chickens do not produce,
they will be sold at market.

I wake up into a brutal world,
a smell of fresh manure
I must rake into a wagon, spread upon the fields.

Each day, I'm awake before light yawns across the world,
and the grass is abundantly green or flattening
and brown before winter. And I'm just getting started.

The sun lolly-gags over the horizon,
stretching its arms of clouds.
I have no time for slowness, no shaking-slumber shoulders,
no dawdling, no stopping to smell the opening rose buds.

My days blend with ground, seed, rain, and sun,
before light to past twilight. Each day offers
either futility or acts of grace. I work until night
is a black stain across the sky with stars
spread across the endless sky
like fields of corn, peas, wheat, and broccoli.
The moon is a sliced apple.

My world fills
with cow bells following the same worn-down path
their ancestors created, time-plodded hard,
back to the barn, back to their own creation.

I don't need a city's fireworks
when at night, fireflies drift their lazy, twinkling flashes,
across the rest of the night, pointing towards
tomorrow with the rooster-weathervane on my barn.

I listen to the land.
The land tells me what I need to know,
how to know it
with all of my senses.

The land tells me
I belong.

Meditations on Hayden's *The Last Seven Words of Christ*

Written in 1786

1. Introduction: Maestoso ed adagio (D minor)

The church walls are covered by black canvas of night
to hush the star's string quartet
so that we do not have to hear their immense grief
in the ominous key of D minor.
Only a single lit lamp hangs in the center rafter —
a moon; a lily; a white garment — to witness
a terrible and trembling world.
The music reveals unimaginable pain.

The earth laments *what will happen next,*
asking, *what have you done?* Trees send out roots
to hold the land together so it will not tear apart
in agony. The land transcends into sheets of music,
into whispers of crickets
playing traumatized green music —
the struggle of someone carrying their own cross.

At this moment, a person is lost, alone,
trapped within a sense of alienation,
accented by the deep tones of a cello, sound rushing in
when the world turns against us —
a world of El Greco shadows,
jagged edges of harsh judgement,
a spine-chill knowing the inevitable.

We can hardly speak.

2. Largo: Father, forgive them, for they know not what they do *(B-flat major)*

We are foolish.
We often cannot see what is in front of us.
Forgive us. When we are scared,
we make mistakes out of our fear of the unknown.
Sometimes, we do not know what we have done
and do not know how it affects others. Forgive us.
When we realize our mistake,
it is difficult to correct later,
and forgiveness does not mean forgetting.
We lose trust when we hurt someone.

Sometimes, it is impossible to correct the damage.
We cannot see their pierced wounds,
not even when their bodies sigh a stream of hurt.

How many times can we forgive?
This is the riddle of all dreams.

Forgive us if we cannot forgive.
Forgive the unforgiveable.
We call out to the divine
hidden in the lavender horizon, requesting tenderness.

An ominous music inside swells —
a hurricane
containing the words "father" and "forgive" —
a language being suffocated while dying,
trying to say something important.

We struggle with the word, "Forgive."

3. Grave e cantabile*: Today shalt thou be with me in paradise*
(C minor, C major)

The good thief knew how to seek forgiveness.
He asked.
He could have been denied.
He could have been ignored.
He was forgiven because he simply asked.

The other thief mocked and insulted like the crowd.
He taunted and died still cursing the world.
But the good thief knew what to do:

he asked.

4. Grave: Woman, behold thy son *(E major)*

During war, the wounded die,
calling for their mothers. No one can save them.

I try patching a wound,
but so many are dying,
panicking and seeing their own deaths,
calling for their mommies like feverous children.

In their moments of weakness, I have to decide
which men I can save and which will die.

Mother: behold
your children dying,
slowly surrendering to death.

Their pain is the sacred fire spoken by a cello's strings.

5. Largo: My God, my God, why hast thou forsaken me? *(E-Flat major)*

We all have moments of weakness.
We can feel abandoned, forgotten,
wounded, wondering where to find help,
feeling we do not deserve help,
ashamed to ask for help.

We all want to find our way to home
where we are welcome.
Sometimes, the door is locked,
and no one answers,
no matter how loudly we pound the door.
No one responds,
turning a deaf ear to our requests.

6. Adagio: I thirst *(A major)*

There's a deeper purple bruise
when wells run dry, when the world rings
with leaping flames.

My thirst dreams of quivering mornings,
flooding with light from within us. I thirst
for a swivel in seas when tides flush
against the shores, and the world is cleansed.
By morning, all the birds will thirst for songs,
and at day's end, their drunken heart-songs
sink beyond the horizon
where the light is combed away with the waves.

Towards their end, a person dying will ask for water.

I thirst for another day, another heartbeat,
another chance to love. Endlessly, I thirst,

while magpies mimic and mock my song,
my thirsty arms try to hold every moment
before it all ends. All I do is empty like a lake.
All I do is cast my net into the world
fishing for some hope. All I do is pull in
nets of dry silence.

7. Lento: It is Finished *(G minor, G major)*

When the dying surrender,
they see the world beyond this one.
Their body tries to release every regret;

but some clench anger, some fight back
at unresolved issues. Some only see a void,
a horrible emptiness of their life.
Some look at their lives with a wry smile,
its mathematical inevitability.

Sometimes, someone dying doesn't finish
what they are saying, words trail off,
comets leaving dust behind them.

My deaf father swore he heard birds before he died.

8. *Largo:* Father, into thy hands I commend my spirit. *(E-flat major)*

A friend stared into his death,
stared through me as if I was not there,
trying to tell me what he was seeing,
fumbling with words, "I can't even…"

And then — a violin surge —
he was gone — blankness in his eyes,
mouth disabled. A bleep of a heart monitor
flattened into a landscape without him.

I held his hand,
trying to hold onto his departure.

I know from all the dying in Vietnam
that once the body dies, it releases slowly.
Lights go out in the body, one by one,
like turning off lights in a house.
It takes longer for the body to go cold as a stone,

I have witnessed many journeys —
some ended abruptly;
some had a long, lingering process—
each was a variation theme in music,
but they all had the same conclusion:
the math is against us;
once the conductor lowers his baton,
the music ends.

After we buried my friend,
his dog lay on top of his grave for a week.
We all have ways to mourn.

9. Coda: Il terremoto: The earth shook, and the rocks split (C minor)

When grieving, some people tremor
a quiet earthquake.
I never know what to say to them.
We tend to see our own inevitable death
when we attend a funeral.

I have witnessed too much death.
I have placed a black flag on my car,
turn on my headlights to mark their passing,
driving in a slow line to their graves.
I've carried their caskets over crushed pebbles,
a lawn so freshly mowed,
the smell of wet, cut grass, lingers,
a green of mourning and resolution.

I have spread ashes in unmarked places.
I have held someone sobbing,
feeling their pain crack lighting.
I've watched the survivors go home
to face the empty place where someone once sat.
I never know what to say.
There are no words that can replace a person.
I never know what to say.

There is no resurrection in this music.
Just a coda when light diminishes.
Just sobbing in the night canvas.
Just a song no bird wants to sing.

After the concert is over,
there's a large emptiness when no one is clapping.

ABOUT MARTIN WILLITTS, JR.

Martin Willitts Jr is a Quaker, and a retired Librarian and former musician living in Syracuse, New York. He was nominated for 17 Pushcart and 13 Best of the Net awards.

 Winner of the 2012 Big River Poetry Review's William K. Hathaway Award; 2013 Bill Holm Witness Poetry Contest; 2013 "Trees" Poetry Contest; 2014 Broadsided award; 2014 Dylan Thomas International Poetry Contest; Rattle Ekphrastic Challenge, June 2015, Editor's Choice; Rattle Ekphrastic Challenge, Artist's Choice, November 2016, Stephen A. DiBiase Poetry Prize, 2018; Editor's Choice, Rattle Ekphrastic Challenge, December, 2020; 17th Annual Sejong Writing Competition, 2022. He won two Central New York Individual Artist Awards and provided "Poetry on The Bus" which had 48 poems in local buses including 20 bi-lingual poems from 7 different languages. He edited two local poetry anthologies under two other Central New York Arts Grants, his most recent was about ecology with poetry, essays, and further reference materials.

Martin Willitts Jr is an editor for the *Comstock Review*, plus judge for the New York State Fair Poetry Contest. He has won numerous poetry awards. He has 21 full-length collections including the Blue Light Award 2019, *The Temporary World*. His recent book is *Not Only the Extraordinary are Exiting the Dream World* (Flowstone Press, 2022). Forthcoming is *Ethereal Flowers* (Shanti Press, 2023). He has appeared numerous times in *Nine Mile Magazine*. His recent poems appear in *Two Hawks Quarterly, Presence, Rise*

Up Review, Paterson Review, Contrary Magazine, Nixes Mate Review and others.

ABOUT THE POEMS

I was a never-fit-in person, beginning at five when I suddenly played piano without instructions. After that, math, science, and music came easily to me. I was performing difficult math equations in elementary school that belonged in senior high school and college.

I'd often told teachers my love of math arrived from music. This was a half-truth, because I saw numbers in terms of music notes or in terms of color. It was not until recently that I understood it was an actual diagnosis for what I did naturally. The term places me on the autism scale. This is the source for the poem, "Math Savant."

Music came to me just as easily. I could scan a sheet of classical music, and I had it committed to memory. I was good enough to play with the Syracuse Symphony at the age of seven. I understood the Latin words for how to play the piece on piano or harpsichord or organ. I could barely reach the foot pedals intended for dampening or increasing volume. I knew how to tie a bow tie. A music background is the source for my poem, "Meditations on Hayden's *The Last Seven Words of Christ.*"

My ADD had a different outlet besides music. Every summer I would visit my Amish and Mennonite grandparents' farm. There I would be kept busy, using all my boundless energy for good purpose. I was up before light and went to bed when it was dark. I saw tons of sunrises, sunsets, star constellations, the effect of light and shadow. In the Amish Meeting House, I had to learn to sit totally still for an hour and a half in silence.

All this is to explain my four poems, "The Filly," "Harvesting Corn," "I Start Before the Sun Wakes Up," and

"Why Love Does Not Need Restrictions. I learned different ways to love on the farm, but I also found a way to resolve my frantic energy with my love of music, math, and science. I practice gentleness with many of the farm animals or planting seed, or watching the sky changing and the earth yielding.

I keep writing to find out what I want to say. I write in silence after silent meditation. I place my chaos into the poetry and let it settle. I hope I have something worthwhile to convey. As an old-fashion oral story, it is important to end the traditional African way: *a story, a story, let it come, let it go.*

George Saitoh

Generational Drift

together we shall withstand
the aches of old age—
redder and more
transparent skin, whiter
knuckles, the boss
of sensory decline;
the hoards of groomed
humans coming to supper
uninvited
(and angry in advance)—
until all slips are foreseen
and all else becomes a receding
dot
   of light years, coning
      towards nebulae
         on the Pillars of Creation,
   where the strangest
      stars are being born.

Stretcher Me Out

You know what they don't say about choices:
choosing eliminates them, leads to a cutout
of one's own making.

Procrastination is one word for holding off choosing,
for paddling in the saltwater shallows among
elucent and tinted boats of possibility

until the system of relations—you and your
choices—snaps shut.

   Now irreversibly

diving through the sharkish protovision:
anonymous memory
                    of silent grey blocks.

ABOUT GEORGE SAITOH

George Saitoh's fiction, essays, poetry and drama have appeared in The Tangerine, Clarion, Aeqai, Kyoto Journal, Healing Muse, Word Riot, Santa Ana River Review, Janus Head, Gravel, Literary Orphans and elsewhere. Hisplays have been performed in Tokyo and Dublin. Born in Dublin he was

educated there and in England. He lives in Tokyo and regularly spends time in Massachusetts.

ABOUT THE POEMS

Stretcher Me Out

In SMO, joy is found in the possession of choices, and deferring a decision; in remaining in the littoral and liminal zone where perceptions of difference (source of learning and wonder) are richest. But it is also a position of oscillating feelings, infantile impotence and anxiety over generational drift. Meanwhile, sharks maraud; you heard they took your ancestors but not how.

Generational Drift

One learns during a human lifespan that reframing of context is a tool for survival and growth when faced with difficulty. In GD, contextual expansion is a distraction from the recording of physical decline. Impending death and social alienation push the searching mind to the edge of the universe, towards an infinite regress. Somewhere here the common thread lies, because it must.

Raymond Luczak

Drying

There is no such thing as walking a straight line
among the dunes. Each step is a tremor rippling outward
in sand. The sun is a knife. Needles bloom like flowers.
You can't stand upright. Your shoulders are boulders.
The sweat once caked in the comfort of your feet
has evaporated. The skin of your soles
have cracked. It hurts to wriggle your toes.
Everything on you feels like onion skin. A breeze
could strip away the last rags of your confidence.
You just need to pay attention. Pay attention! God.
Your tongue has become a parchment crumbling
into the madness of moisture. You are dry inside.
How you wish you could float like a Steadicam,
a glissando among the wind, a forgiving salve.

Thermography

If we were forced to pose together for a photograph, we didn't shake hands.

Distance, preferably a continent or two away, was our idea of summer warmth.

Whenever we met on the street, it was always winter.

Not the dreary weather kind punctured with lonely trees, but the really ugly kind.

The nightmarish kind that whips Antarctica in the bellows of midnight.

Like king penguins clustered in a circle, we kept our smiles tight like band-aids on our faces.

If we nodded acknowledgment at all, it was at least -133 Fahrenheit degrees.

We resisted the temptation to slingshot insults at each other.

Nothing we wore was warm enough to insulate from the pain of each other.

Even small talk was water torture.

We left behind a trail of hot coals daring the other to walk barefoot.

Hearing the other yelp was satisfying.

We turned away if we happened to overhear gossip about each other.

Yet we dreamed of no one else.

Our surreptitious snapshots of each other showed our hearts throbbing in the same color.

ABOUT RAYMOND LUCZAK

Raymond Luczak is the author and editor of over 30 books, including *Lunafly* (Gnashing Teeth), *Chlorophyll*

(Modern History Press), and *Far from Atlantis* (Gallaudet University Press, forthcoming). His work has appeared in *Poetry*, *Prairie Schooner*, and elsewhere. An inaugural Zoeglossia Poetry Fellow, he lives in Minneapolis, Minnesota.

ABOUT THE POEMS

My two poems here were an attempt to play more with the idea of depicting *sensation*. The poem "Drying" was more about motion, and the other poem "Thermography" explored the dynamics between heat and distance, particularly between two people who hate each other and yet still ache for each other. You could say that it was a "thought experiment."

Mark DeCarteret

The Year We Went Without a Dog

for Bill and Nancy

We remembered being told. How she wouldn't get any
older. How her big orange mouth. She'd eventually let drop at
our feet. Where it would turn. Mostly to light. And how when
the mouth felt the need to laugh. She'd end up with. A
thousand sticks for each tooth. Or a thousand kittens tugged
out from a fire. And we were told how her big orange mouth
would soon turn into a gold. That would be difficult to take in.
Or refer to. Especially when the sun was unseasonably cold.
At its furthest south. And how certain insects. Might form a
team around. Where her mouth smelled like tedium. And meat.
Her dented up dish. Sounding off as if amplified. Underlined
in black ink. And how anybody who had touched the dog. But
more often a child. Would be clicked into being. Like a replica
of the dog. Everything but her mouth. And the smell of the
meat. And how there was nothing. Her mouth wouldn't trade
for a good shell. Or the sand that it harbored. Something
unstrung like the sun. And all it nosed out of the room. If the
sky was all taken. How when she would see the need to laugh.
Or unveil something gray in the water. Perhaps a seal. Or the
remains of a boat. It would be altered by salt. And wind-dried
into a different form. Of beauty. For was there anything the
dog wouldn't kiss? Or commit to her mouth? Till she was sad-
eyed and sick. And so heavy with sighs. She would finally let
her soul stream across the sky. That sky that once held its own.
In a series of unremarkable skies.

The Year I Went Without Listening to the Kid's Kiddie Music

And if they stare
Just let them burn their eyes
On you moving
—"Hold Your Head Up"

I picked old food off of my shirt. Egg from Wednesday. Rice from Friday. This sugary cereal, milk, from whenever. All of it keeping rather nicely. And then tirelessly watched clips of me reciting "Changes in my Privacy Policies." I also folded these window-scapes into eighths again. So that the snow, white as packing material, would wander out into the woods. Potentially never to be seen again. Fields would be super-sized. As per my chant. Each grass-blade a lost soul, a saga. And entire seas would be lost to the creases. Later sung about in an Icelandic ardency. I'm often depicted as a kind of human softening agent, a fool. With a perpetual thirst for arriving. As a child I swung a neighbor around by the cape into the wet earth. Where he'd dismiss his soiled knees with a chivalrous shrug. To be fair, he first came at me with his arm cast. On which I had written in volcanic red marker—"May our friendship never come to this." Now this is all I bring to the group share. Burden this flip pad of sky. On the wallpaper, dolphins approach my boat with offers of safe passage. Always snickering and fin-clapping. Bending aristocratically from the waist. I feel tacky and cast off in their midst. Ignored at the dollar store. Nowadays, I wound so easily. Grow cross and sore in the joints from this effort to break free from the world. At a virtual conference I once asked Tom Lux to borrow his golden lever. Instead, winding up with an inflatable bell. That I'd bring to the surface when I felt any come on of self-mockery. Years later, I can't work up the breath. Only this image of him. Dancing in widening circles to Argent.

The Year I Went Without Parkinson's

My father didn't so much pray over me. Drop down on the floor and play God. As to get out his tools. Try to repair where I'd developed this leak. And my mother didn't so much get out her sewing kit. Stick me with needles. As to aim ray guns at the sides of my neck. Stun this alien life. As it made for my head. There is no reason to be afraid, they both said. But if you need to be. We'd understand. And so, I disappeared into the pair of them. Where my heart had first looked to me for some word. And my tears had their start. And then I ran from the world, Lord. O how I ran.

The Year I Went Without Shutting My Eyes

Yet another draft. Where some winged thing. Takes leave
of heaven. Only to be trapped in the rafters. One is designed
either to. Laugh it all off. Or to fall in with the early light.
Where White Island appears. Farther from shore than the day
before. Still, the waves are reassuring us. Even though the boat
cannot see us. Not every note needs to be sung. So, one rounds
off an orange rind of sun. But then leaves behind the shadows
on the entertainment center. Convincing us we've uncovered a
Motherwell. Most days we are wed more to that one most
dubious of boasts. Than we are thousands of credible doubts.
Maybe this is why you sound more like the wind in the wires
than the wind in the wires. Now, let's rewind to where several
stars. Have burned down to nubs on the ground. And then
cooled into the blackest of buttons. Look at us sweeping them
into piles. Sweep, sweep. Sweep, sweep. Did I tell you that--
Rexroth texted me again? The easiest answers are only found.
He insisted. In the easiest questions. Well, well, that's just
swell. In the meantime, seven of these seals are inconsolable,
wet-eyed. And they've traveled years underwater just to see
me. So, your voice is getting smaller and smaller. With too
much mouth to fit it in. He keeps letting me know. As if I'd
tapped out the wonder. My curiosity no longer visible from
space. Like that cell tower. Or illuminated visor. I'm trying too
hard not to make. Any more of a scene. Now the words only
heard from the inside. This masterwork as formless and
ungovernable as love. One eagle per glance. And so few
swans, one can count them on one's folding hand. As a child
on the edge of sleep I dared myself. To walk through the only
door. Without any sign. The question is Kenneth. Is it the door
that fails us. Or are we failing the door? If this is not the
answer you sought, he keeps reminding me. Then take it up
with the river. Take it up with the river.

The Year I Went Without Deliciousness

This time it's all the tears. I wouldn't allow to intervene.
Now, eating me at my will. She in that state again. I always
saw. As at-sea. And as a waste of both water and salt. The next
time, it'll be the sea itself. Sun-stroked and accosted.
Unreasonably massive. Rather we'd come to rest in the
mockup of forest. Or under the spell of rooftops and
storefronts. The candy-assed come on of some lap dance. O
love, it's been lifetimes since I tasted Ritsos' olives on your
lips. Only the pills. The false mint of your toothpaste. And the
truths it still hints at. The instant we pull apart. All through
breakfast, the cardinal's song assails me. Like some spirit
being lured out into the light. Or some even murkier thing
being cradled by night. Let me tell you, they make one hell of
an omelet here. The only time I tried out. For the biopic they
made of my life. It was only for a bit part. I'd wear prosthetic
teeth. And a fright wig. Never seeing myself as the star. Or
even their stunt double. Figuring only in the scene. Where I
grieve for our founders' loss. How unsound it's become. Yes.
those Vikings sure got around. But all the credit goes out to
their boats. Their ingestion of certain fats. For me, even the
fur-lined boots are a tough sell. The dried-out meat that I keep
in the pantry. That come six to a box. All that's left is my
velvety likeness. And the twelve imposters they used for my
headshot. Do these antlers make me look thinner? Does armor
make me look cool? One can't recant what one can't recall
canting at all can one. But as a good sport she's a pro. To the
point where she stopped making a case for my deportation.
Starting up my own nation. For what seems like an eternity
I've sat by the sea. Sipping broth. And then pissing it out.
That's as close as I get, Ritsos. To taking a trip. Or to
composing a poem. At this age, you start seeing it all as the
same. Loud and dull. Little hitting the spot. Has you losing

your shit. Till one is brought back as the memory. Of a
memory. Resisting even the fingertips. The words that it takes.
To work up a spit. All that's left of that self. One felt ashamed
of. In name only. We should kiss while we remember to, love.
While there's air, sweet with youth, in our lungs. And olives,
salty with flesh, on our tongues.

The Year I Went Without Seeing Through the Floaters

They tumble-weeded into town. And were harassed by the ghosts. Learning nearly all there was to learn. From the lake that dried up. The skeleton of a cow. They were fitted for gowns. And vowed to devote entire works to me. They bowed over in pain. But stopped short of worshipping it. As hard as I tried, they would never really grow on me. Nor would I get the right wording. For all their dealings with night. They hand-shadowed crows on a sheet we'd hanged down from the ceiling fan. And then feasted for days where the neighbors had mown. The dust more light than light. They knew nothing of what we thought we had known. And everything about what we knew we had thought. Mornings, they posted the Dow. And evenings, hosted parties they couldn't even pretend to afford. They lowered the heavens by a foot or two. Using leftover pullies and cords. They reaped some. They sowed more. In voices thrown into an undertaker's suit. How it sounded like thunder. A county or so in the distance.

ABOUT MARK DECARTERET

Poems from Mark DeCarteret's manuscript *The Year I/We Went Without* have been taken by *The American Poetry Review, Asheville Poetry Review, BlazeVOX, The Ekphrastic Review, Gargoyle, Guesthouse, Hole in the Head Review, Map Literary, Meat for Tea, Nixes Mate Review, On the Seawall, Plume, Saw Palm, South Florida Poetry Journal, SurVision, Turtle Island Quarterly, Unbroken* and *Unlost.*

ABOUT THE POEMS

It was February. At a workshop in Delray. And the heat, if not the humidity, remembers Tom Lux saying. He couldn't be bothered with stanzas anymore. That they were no longer worth the trouble. Maybe even too fine, and extravagant, a thing. Ten years later and I'd start to feel the same about lines. That they'd become over thought, worked. In love with only themselves. Merely decorous. And that I'd rather crowd the page with them. Keep getting in another last word. Involve even more of the world. Leaving the commercial breaks. To the clowns up in the booth. And so, I'd throw my voice in. With some Parisian mime. And that sorry-assed prose poem. A series of them I'd repeatedly title "The Year I/We Went Without." Where I would seemingly get free of the line's endless needs. Having had enough of its aging strides. Low-in-fat diet phrases. Its sluggish turns. Gulps of air. Its sudden dusting offs, shuddering. Its fussing over and suffering. The same ache, the same chair. And the same hidden fees. But instead of a maze-like case against symmetry. A breathless recreation of meter's death. A scream of no discernible make. A big sack of chaos. Or the same mess that mime and I rode in on. I'd find myself just as lyrically minded. Still given to song. The tune I'd once noted as gone. Still periodically dropping in. Refereeing each snap. With both an ear and an eye on the time clock. This measure of life. Still wired for what will never sit well. And the fits of stiff-jointed flight. The diminished melodies of the past. Half in awe of the future. Half laughing it off. And the tension-filled tradeoffs. Between the letting it rest. For a spell. And the retelling of it. Lest we sleep.

Jeanne Julian

Nonsense

The yoga teacher's murmured cue
does not make sense:
Breeeeathe down the spine
through the pelvis into Mother Earth.
Yet, as you and I, strangers, rest
aligned side by side in corpse pose
here on this worn linoleum floor,
imagination instills a sensual stability.

Wonderful the way simplistic non-sense
works upon us. For good—
as when, inhaling, we feel grounded
on this planet's unseen surface.
Or for ill—as when the gullible swallow
ballyhoo and call the slaughtered
crisis actors, because it makes no sense
that someone gunned down children.

Preposterous heaven—sky-haven populous
with crisis-actor angels—is nonsensical
as Oz but gives collective comfort.
Likewise, some say shenanigans of the moon,
its hide-and-seek, its halos, might govern
our moods. Or, perhaps the zodiac
at your birth sparked your character, charted
a life course for you to follow or defy.

Are such allegations lunacy?
Or maybe they hold some logic mislaid
when we lost our senses, lost

our willingness to trust the cycles
of our cosmos. So we grow strawberries
in January, add sand to beaches,
suck wetlands dry. Breathtaking,
how we hack away at our own roots.

How little sense it makes.

Yogic ritual completed, we sigh,
deeply. And curling like spring ferns,
we turn—
onto our right sides, as if offering
our hearts, those impulse-driven
muscles caged in bone, to the universe.
As if opening our selves to possibility,
sensible or not.

Heaven on Earth

St. Peter's Basilica, Vatican City

A handful of euros buys their ticket to the top.
Tucked behind the splendid loot of the basilica—
athletic saints, carved altar canopy with undulant pillars,
golden roulette-wheel window centered with a dove—
is the small, stark *ascensore*, an elevator operated
by a businesslike young man in a blue suit.
"St. Peter as bodyguard," she whispers, "or 007."
With him they glide upward to the overarching vault,

the astonishing dome of indigo and gold:
"A grifter's shell-game cup on a grand scale,"
he says. "Think of all the cash locked up in faith."
As they edge along the balcony, brushing past
mosaic walls—from afar, subtle as paintings;
up close, labor-intensive chips of gleam and glitter—
their American gaze takes in vast marble chapels,
red-clad officiants, worshippers tiny as bugs.

The vertiginous view aggravates his fear of heights.
They exit to the rooftop. Here's a New World order,
the inverse of heaven on earth: café, souvenir stand,
a Ladies' and Men's (but just holes in the floor),
papal post office, and a rear view the of guardian statues
who survey the plaza far below: huge, antique, holy
humans, saints fractured, patched, and propped,
iron straps, braces, and prostheses invisible from below.

"And so the grand illusion is maintained."
Later, when their dusty shoes push off
from the airport tarmac to board the flight

through the firmament back to their home state,
an earthquake ripples all around old Rome.
Did their last irreverent steps on fragile empire
tip the balance, venerable land shuddering in recoil?
Or did they just escape some divine rebuke?

ABOUT JEANNE JULIAN

Jeanne Julian is the author of *Like the O in Hope* (The Poetry Box, 2019) and two chapbooks. Her poems appear in *Poetry Quarterly, Panoply, Snapdragon, Kakalak, Ocotillo Review, MacQueen's Quinterly* and other journals and have won awards from *Reed Magazine* (co-winner, Edwin Markham Prize 2019), *The Comstock Review, Naugatuck River Review*, and Maine Poets' Society. She regularly reviews poetry books for *The Main Street Rag*. Jeanne lives in South Portland, Maine. www.jeannejulian.com

ABOUT THE POEMS

Statement about 2 poems: Both poems have to do with belief systems. "Nonsense" is meant to move from a delight in self-delusion, which can be a comfort, to a frustration with self-delusion of all kinds, especially in our short-sighted treatment of the planet. "Heaven on Earth" is rooted in the contrast between Old World and New, a tension that's been there from *Letters from an American Farmer* through Henry James.

Nancy Jean Hill

Hypnagogia

I see them when my eyes are shut.
During the time between awake and asleep.
Some are strangers; some are not.
Coming through my eyelids
in squares and circles, or flipping
on the screen like a slideshow.
Never in black and white.

Last night, my Aunt Glenna appeared,
sitting up proudly in her wheelchair.
How loudly and terribly off-key
she sang to her nursing-home friends.
You are my sunshine, my darling sunshine.
 How she loved the microphone, the audience.

Sometimes, I see my own image.
Black-rimmed glasses,
white-bobbed hair, blue, blue eyes.
Not what I see in the mirror
these days, a face so blurry and distorted,
I have given up trying to apply lipstick.

I saw my father the other night,
Sitting on the Sheridan Street
patio in a webbed lawn chair.
A glass of bourbon in his hand, no ice.
He wore a brown checkered shirt
And a smirk.

A hideous, red-headed clown
visits much too often.
Like my father, he smirks.
He stays for a long time.
When he finally leaves,
soft-eyed people appear,
one right after another,
wearing clothing from past centuries.
And I am relieved.
I know I am drifting into sleep.
And I fear no evil.

Watering Daffodils

I am walking my dog when I see a woman watering daffodils
with a sprinkling can that looks much too heavy for her to
 carry.

She is my neighbor, though I must hike up a steep hill through
 the woods
to get to her house and the street she lives on is not the same as
 mine.

She wants to know my name, and I tell her.
She tells me hers, which I immediately forget.

She tells me she is downsizing.
"I am eighty-seven years old, and this is too much!"

I wonder what she means by too much. Watering daffodils?
Carrying the heavy can up the hill?

"Are you selling?" I ask.
 Selling and moving to a smaller home is my idea of
 downsizing.

"Oh, no!" she exclaims.
"If we sold, we'd have to live in our car."

I have no idea to whom the "we" refers
but I presume she has a husband living still.

She tells me about her kids: all retired or about to.
Grandkids: no more interest in coming to the lake.

"I'm just getting rid of things," she explains. "I used to think
  it was awful
to throw everything into a dumpster, but now I understand
  why people do it."

I am getting antsy, and the dog needs to poop
so I walk away, while asking her to repeat her name.

"Mary Bouchard", she says, and I can tell she expects me to
  know who she is
and all about the important town committees she once chaired.

"Mary Bouchard," I repeat out loud, my new technique for
  holding on to names.
"Oh, don't try to memorize it," she says. "I'll be dead by
  then."

I am distressed by the impending death of this woman
whose name I know I shall soon forget.

She sees my grief. Tries to comfort me.
"Oh, don't worry," she says. "Dying. It's a lot easier than
  living."

ABOUT NANCY JEAN HILL

Nancy Jean Hill's chapbook, *Beryllium Diary*, was first published by Pudding House Press in 2007 and reprinted by  Igneus Press in 2015. Her full-length collection of poetry, *Unholy Ghost*, was published by Kelsay Books in 2016. Recently, her poem, *"Snorkeling"* received an honorable mention from *Passager*'s 2022 Poetry Contest. Her poems have also appeared in several literary journals, including *Calyx; Phoebe; Notes Magazine; Omphalos; Slipstream; Tower Journal; Café Review;* and *Hole in the Head Review.* She lives and writes in Exeter, New Hampshire and Readfield, Maine.

ABOUT THE POEMS

Watering Daffodils: When I was a very young woman, I found myself studying older people and wondering about them. I suppose my curiosity was also a fear, knowing that I, too, was destined to grow old. Seniors are often unseen, but I continue to observe people who are older than me. I learn from them. Although the woman in this poem seems somewhat resigned to her situation, there is also a sense of acceptance and peace.

Hypnagogia: I don't know when this started, but at some point, I began having random visions before falling asleep. I thought maybe this was a common experience, so I asked my husband if the same thing happened to him. When he said "no", I did some research and found that there is an actual phenomenon called hypnagogia. As I read more about it, I was inspired to write this poem,

William Welch

Dead Horse Bay

Do not walk barefoot here.
The sand is strewn with glass.
Ruinous and inchoate at once, the shoreline recedes
toward Rockaway. March. Wind
spits rain at the ocean's face.
Gulls hover in a landward breeze. At the edge of the beach,
above the tide's limit, seven-foot tall reeds form a cane-break,
dry, brittle, soughing. I have entered
a flowerbed of bones.

A hundred years ago, Manhattan sent its chattel here,
old animals, no longer capable of work,
the wounded, the obstinate.
Butchers slaughtered horses
by the thousands. They dumped offal
into the bay, but tide by tide the sea returned their offering.
Crouching, I find white blossoms
growing out of the sand—ribs, pasterns, pieces of a horse's
    knee.
This cemetery the butchers made
has become a garden.

Nearby, moss-carpeted boards form floors, a driftwood house
without walls, without a roof.
Careful of where I step, feeling
one moment I'm intruding, the next, proprietary,
I walk from room to room.

When the rendering plants closed, the city used this place
as a landfill—as though we expected the sea

to remember our lives for us,
to clean away our history.
Both what we loved and what we disowned,
what we brought to life, and what we tried to drown. ´
Just as the sea returned the horses,
it returns our garbage. Half-buried
dinner plates, shattered, shine through the sand.
Cough syrup bottles, old jars
filled with pebbles roll forward in a wave,
roll back. Water dabs its salve
across the cheeks of a ceramic doll, its skull lying broken
beside oyster shells. The ribs of a derelict
yacht lie keel-over in a dune,
as if the makeshift sea were a junk dealer
fashioning a model for a modern whale.
And shoes. Hundreds, some reduced to their soles,
others intact, even with laces, step forward
from the surf, as if a whole city
of men and women, like myself,
were stepping out of the calm waves,
followed by a shadow of birds.

*

Distant enough from Brooklyn,
there are only three sounds here—
the sound of rain pelting sand,
the sound of wind in dry grass,
the sound of water washing over glass.
Small waves, delicate, curled,
like a boy's fingers arched
over piano keys, chime
glass against glass. Accidental music.
I remember this.

I remember sitting at the keyboard on summer afternoons, the
    song book
closed, pressing keys down
so gently, the hammers only made the strings tremor rather
    than resound.
What my hands played,
I heard, unsure if the music was in the piano,
or in me, or if it traveled through an open window
missing half its notes—a song
someone else was rehearsing in another house.
I listened, trying to recognize a melody,
until I crossed the point at which the hammers touched the
    strings
without making a sound.

That was not music
I could play again, or play just once.
It was not a text notated,
bearing time signature, and key.
I could not reproduce it then,
but recognize it now. Intuition insists
this is what I heard. Knowledge is reproducible, intuition
is not. Knowledge depends on time,
intuition recognizes time to be
a house with many rooms, whose windows overlook separate
    streets...
We look through, we say time has a single outcome,
but intuition implies time
takes every direction, not only one. Look again,
choose a different window...

*

The water moves back,
pauses,
rushes forward—
a respiration. Each breath brings out another note.

I walk close to the cane-break, listening.
Wind moves through the reeds,
bending, snapping them.
There is no sign yet of any regaining green.

All around are traces of what this place was,
or what it will be. It is confusing
to stand here, to wonder if those are my shoes
washed up by storm surge,
if I am one of the butchers walking home after work, a man
who smells iron everywhere, the stench of rotting meat.
I think about my life, how it may be
a perversion of sacrifice—
the sea, god of horses, received their blood,
not as tribute, but out of convenience.
I picture the water blossoming, becoming a greenhouse of
    poinsettias,
imagine the rocks clotted, the waves frothy with albumin…
I think about how we abuse our own bodies,
lead people into the killing room.
What escape is there? Where would I go if I could get away?

Closer to the surf, the sand is covered with thick mats of
    seaweed,
kelps, and thin grasses. A few tires,
and rubber skirts from traffic drums lie scattered around.
What if I walk down to the water?

If I follow the horses in?
What kind of return
would the tide bring about?

It takes faith
to put corn and squash into the ground,
to hope the seeds grow. What faith
those men laboring in the slaughterhouse had,
to plant bones in the sea!
One day, the crop of new horses will come,
the whinny of a wave announcing them.

I kneel, a gardener among his calcium roses.
I pick one white flower,
a blossom to carry with me,
a boutonnière.

One of Those Guys

in memory of Gerald Stern

You've known one of those guys,
haven't you? The one who brings the heavy
subjects into every conversation?
He always starts with a casual remark,
if odd, like how he sometimes compares
himself to a moth—not really
in the spirit-animal way—and not
an adult moth so much as a caterpillar.
You think, oh, ha ha, a self-deprecating
joke, I got you bro, but before you can
smooth out the grin, he's broached
all the "issues," from the problem of love,
to the blunders of Congress, and
has even made references to
Talmudic exegesis, all without taking
a breath, all while holding a cup of coffee
the barista overfilled—and you can't help
wondering how on earth he's going
to get that all the way to his mouth
without spilling it. What's even more
impressive is the steadiness
of his hands, because he will hold
that overfull cup still for half an hour
while he steers your discussion from
Shakespeare's identity to neoliberal capitalism
and how we've all been convinced
to turn our lives into commercial products...
It's a delicate task, for sure, weaving
this conversation in and out of the road
blocks of small talk and conventional opinion.

Maybe he secretly believes he's a nuisance,
that people take him for a nutty
Cassandra, running around town weeping.
But I wouldn't say that. Because he is funny,
and warm—someone I'm always
glad to see, although afterwards I'm a little sore,
as though I'd been lifting crates of books,
or holding a two-by in place, waiting
for my partner to drive a screw into the wood.
It's a kind of pain you feel all over
and take some amount of pride in because
you can say you got something done…
Just the other day, I was telling a friend
of mine about how my wife and I
raised monarchs this summer, from egg
to full-blown butterfly in four weeks—
we had nineteen, in total—and don't you know,
this guy had the nerve to ask me if
I was going to be sad if they went extinct?

ABOUT WILLIAM WELCH

William Welch lives in Utica, NY where he works as a registered nurse. His poetry has appeared in various journals,

recently in *Little* Patuxent *Review, The Decadent Review,* and *Offcourse*. His poem "Xoc/Shark" was nominated for a Best of the Net by *Rust+Moth*. He edits *Doubly Mad* for The Other Side of Utica (doublymad.org).

ABOUT THE POEMS

These two poems seem on the surface to be very different from one another when I read them, but they are linked by a common ethical concern that runs throughout much of my work. "Dead Horse Bay" is a poem I've struggled with for many years, in part because the experience that prompted it was so moving. When I visited the beach, I was awed by the location. There are many places where you can "feel time," or where our sense of time is drawn into question, but that spot in particular was uncanny. It seemed to encapsulate many of our social dilemmas, from the ongoing climate catastrophe, to the breakdown of our social institutions, and so on. A poet who always worked our ethical crises into his work in a sensitive and thought provoking way was Gerald Stern, who passed away late last year. I was unfamiliar with his work before—sadly—but have been binge-reading him over the past couple of months. If you do not know his work, I strongly recommend him! "One Of Those Guys" was prompted by his poem "Persona," which is in his collection *This Time*. Page 280!

Christopher Buckley

Philosophers

Gary DeVito 1947-2007

I still see DeVito's chiseled jaw, the face that was
the spitting image of Hollywood's Gilbert Roland,
his handsome mug that got him out of a hundred jams
in school, and had him thinking he could get away
with anything until the draft notice came.

I was in college struggling with Philosophy 101
while Gary's brain was happily running loose
as rain water in the highlands of Pleiku—
living in a loin cloth with the Montagnards,
smoking that resin-soaked weed, miles beyond
good and evil, and believing most everything
Nietzsche wrote without ever reading a word.
Gary who was existential, but spoke no French,
who didn't know Marx from Machiavelli, but
who'd never fallen in line with middle class
materialism. Gary who was finally taken back
by force-recon guys, who, dark as ghosts, humped it
umpteen klicks up river to haul him out without
his pipe or the chief's daughter whom he'd married
without a second thought.
                                        Gary heard Wagner,
Nietzsche's pal, one time only in Coppola's film,
blasted from helicopters swooping down like Valkyries
on the VC, the way it never happened. And he wasn't
coming back to the world by a long shot, after 30 years
in the Post Office and 5 DUIs.
                                        How many times

now have I wanted to grab Nietzsche by the collars
of his great coat and say, "OK wise guy, where
do all the big ideas get us?"

Schopenhauer was right
about the eternal torment of desire, and he didn't surf;
tug on Spinoza's cloak and he'd never have come up
with anything to save Gary from his last misfortune,
forgetting he was 60, following that young woman
into Motel 6—a little chemical boost for the blood
despite all the tipsy electricity of the heart about to
short out—zap, *muy pronto*—bad luck, free radicals,
karma, or recessive genes . . . pick one.

Emerson
would have advised him to stay put in the jungle
as long as someone was bringing in lunch and
the correspondence.

Gary never picked up on
the fact that he was no superman, that his faculties
could collapse in Carpinteria next to the 101 freeway
as easily as in Turin, in the Piazza Carlo Alberto,
the way Nietzsche's grip on the nature of being slipped
away one afternoon as he threw his arms around
the neck of a horse being whipped, looked into its eyes,
and asked, *My God, why are we so unhappy?*

Last Elegy

Jon Veinberg 1947-2017

Low clouds pierced by evening
light, and a plane rumbling over
unseen spooks a choir of cedar
waxwings in the pyracantha

who depart in a flash—a rush
of air stripping everything but
silence from the bush. I look up
through the gauze, the scramble

of branches and surrender
my speculations, pausing
to think, waiting . . . and look
for you across the rising

prospect and spill of stars
that always whispered to us
about death, that worm in our blood.
Nowhere else to look? Not a clue—

not one dove's grey feather
drifting from a sun-baked sycamore,
not the least sign or wonder in
the dust. Yet, when I close my eyes

I still see you on your porch,
scanning down the block for
one of our *compadres* showing up
late, running low on hope,

bags of it we each carried with us
then. . . . Here, the street ends
at the sea, where there are no more
secrets for the dead to keep.

ABOUT CHRISTOPHER BUCKLEY

Christopher Buckley is editor of *NAMING THE LOST: THE FRESNO POETS*—Interviews *& Essays*, Stephen F. Austin State Univ. Press, 2021. Recent books are, *The Consolations of Science & Philosophy*, Lynx House Press, 2022 and *One Sky to the Next*, winner of the Long Leaf Press Book Prize, due early 2023.

ABOUT THE POEMS

These two poems are both elegies—one for a high school friend from Santa Barbara and the other for my great friend the Fresno Poet Jon Veinberg for whom I wrote several elegies in my book AGNOSTIC, from Lynx House Press in 2019. "Last Elegy" is set on Brown Street, at Jon's house, before his death in 2017. It is supposed to be the last of such elegies, but I don't know. . . .

Since the late '80s I've looked to science and philosophy as touchstones, as corroboration for doubts and speculation—societal and metaphysical—for a base to find a few recoveries and enunciate the loss and wholesale ironies that our lives present.

Annie Snider

Witness

We were looking for something to do
It was cold, so cold
in the hillcountry.
Tired of being inside
We'd read all the Louis L'Amour paperbacks
And played all the backgammon
in front of the big fire.
My 15 year old brother picked up his rifle and headed outside
I went with him
"Stay here" he said quietly
"No!," I said, throwing my leg over the
back seat of the tractor.
"I'm going."
He stared at me for a long moment.
Shrugged.
Got on and we were off.
We chuffed down the winding road,
over cattle guards and slowed for glimpses of
scissortail flycatchers and an armadillo scuttling.
Stopped at a bend to turn the engine off and listen.
The wind chafed my ears, carried messages.
We were downwind, he made sure.
He spotted a deer at the top of the ridge,
pulled out his rifle and placed it on his shoulder.
I stepped off the tractor to watch.
He squinted to see through the scope.
He paused, drew in a breath and pulled the trigger.
The boom shocked the quiet air, a squeal followed,
and DAMNDAMNDAMN
He watched through the scope

"What?! What happened?" I asked.

I started to walk up toward the ridge.

Pulled my coat tighter, the squealing getting higher.

"Annie, no! Come back here!" he said.

I ran faster. When I got to the top, the sound had ceased.

I had to search. I followed the blood.

A doe had pushed her body, minus two front legs

through the undergrowth to a low bush,

where her fawn huddled quivering by her side.

Her huge eyes blinked in terror,

heart pounding the light out of them.

I ran back, "You have to put her out of her misery!"

He walked back and forth in front of the tractor.

The fawn, he said. The fawn will starve.

The fawn will starve either way! I said.

Get on, he said.

I was ten years old.

He wiped tears away as he steered us home.

Don't talk about this, he said.

 We never have.

Johannesburg Afternoon

An expansive yard
    necklaced by a whitewashed cement enclosure
shards of glass dancing along the top.
Purple flowers rioting up the wall
A golden weaver's nest in my hands,
discovered in a low
acacia tree, long abandoned.
Captivated in the cast shadow of the tangling light,
I want to take this gorgeous creation
    home -
across a continent, an ocean, another continent.
How to keep it intact?
The tear-drop shaped chamber holds mysteries for me.
The male weaver bird spent long hours
meticulously binding, knotting,
pursing, pulling, and threading this grass womb,
this fragile shelter from the elements.
The knots he tied are the only known kind that birds make;
this nest rivals the handiwork of my lowcountry Gullah
    Geechee.
Unlike the wall, no glass shards kept predators at bay.
It served a beautiful purpose.
Tiny down feathers still whisper from the cavity.
I knew I had to keep this nest -
    icon of sanctuary in a shredded world.
The woman of the house comes outside,
barks orders at the Dobermans to retreat.
Her eyes narrow: What are you doing with that filthy thing?
I suddenly see that it probably is covered in mites,
minute pests invisible to my naked eye.
I don't care.
I cradle it, take it inside.

ABOUT ANNIE SNIDER

Annie Snider is a teaching artist in the schools with Gemini Ink in San Antonio, Texas. She works with words, found objects, paint, and collage. Poetry is her portal to stories, thoughts and possibilities.

ABOUT THE POEMS

Witness - a memory that comes back every so often. It was violent and heart-breaking, and I never hunted again. I come from a family of hunters, so this created a rupture in my identity away from my family of origin. One that I am not ungrateful for.

Johannesburg Afternoon- I was doing a year of post-grad study in South Africa, and staying briefly with a white family in Joburg. This was right after Mandela came to power, and the white population was scared. I met so many lovely people of all colors but this particular couple in Joburg... they were marinating in fear. It makes me wonder what they did before apartheid ended. Their guilt was palpable.

Stephen Kampa

Face the Music

Can we talk
    about to face the music,
she texts me, not
    because there's music to face
but because we're word persons—word nerds, even—
    and love the unexpected
ripples and tangles of language. *Where does it*
    come from, why would it be bad.
I envision an imperial throne room
    silent except for the soft

insinuations of a septet of string instruments,
    and before the emperor
fidgets some frantic
    low-level functionary
about to discover which finger he will no longer
    be needing, but since I'm next
to my laptop, the network in easy reach, I look it up.
    The *OED*: "[Origin
uncertain and disputed: suggestions include reference
    to a nervous performer

coming onstage in musical theatre, or to the practice
    of drumming a soldier out
of his regiment (see drum v.*1*), or to
    various military
uses of music n. (as e.g. senses 5
    and 8c at that entry).],"
and being a diligent worder, I click on sense
    5, which reads, "that component

of a military force charged with sounding signals
     on musical instruments,"

and I think, *sure,*
     I wouldn't want to face that,
and then I jump
     to 8c: "*slang* (chiefly *Mil.*).
The sound of gunfire or other
     ordnance," and that's all it takes,
I'm thinking of what I've been thinking of for two
     days straight, the man who hammered
out his hotel windows and opened fire on a country
     music festival, killing

more people than any mass shooter in "modern
     American history."
So this is history. People thought
     the gunshots were sound problems
or fireworks. Some of them have now
     become numbers to the rest
of us, parts of an unimaginable sum.
     It happened in Paradise,
an unincorporated (at root: "unembodied") town
     near Las Vegas, a city

enamored of chance, one where you yank the same
     lever over and over,
forever hopeful that here, at long last, your lucky
     numbers will come up, your ship
come in, your cliché
     dreams come true, and despite how
often you lose—how far you are from ever
     hitting the bells-and-whistles
jackpot—you pull
     the lever, you play your hand,

your ship
    always seems almost in sight
of land, and in the midst
    of this it is probably
wrong to be angry at the aggressive stupidity
    of #heartbroken, now
trending in America, except that I am angry:
    the language, or what passes
for language, angers me. Can we talk
    about facing the music,

can we talk about the not-talking
    and the overtalkative,
the shouters-down, the shammers, the spin doctors,
    the czars of twittle-twattle,
can we talk about Twitter? Scroll down a few days and you
    see,
    "Videogames are giving
guys unrealistic standards as to how
    many swords we can carry,"
and then, of course, "#heartbroken," because the language
    we use for videogame

quips is the same
    language we use for human
massacres here in the bumper-sticker nation,
    home of the slogan shogun
with insights bound to wind up sound bites,
    harbor for the hair-triggered
trigger-happy captains of snappy comebacks—
    the woman I saw today
wore a black spaghetti-strap tank that blared
    OBAMA CAN'T TAKE THESE GUNS

just two days after.
　　Our shootings are beginning
to feel like echoes—so many precede them—
　　but unlike most echoes, these
aren't fading:
　　they're growing louder, growing
stronger, sounds
　　amplified after their first
report
　　from some distant, unknown source.

Can we talk? *The Onion*
　　publishes the same headline,
"'No Way To Prevent This,' Says Only Nation Where
　　This Regularly Happens,"
every time this happens.
　　Numbers keep ratcheting up
like a decibel meter reading: the world's too loud
　　to hear. #heartbroken.
Gunfire. We're facing nothing. What we won't say is
　　music to somebody's ears.

ABOUT STEPHEN KAMPA

Stephen Kampa is the author of three collections of poetry: *Cracks in the Invisible, Bachelor Pad*, and *Articulate as Rain*.

His work has appeared in the *Yale Review, Cincinnati Review, Southwest Review, Hopkins Review, Poetry Northwest, Subtropics*, and *Smartish Pace*. He was also included in *Best American Poetry 2018*. During the spring of 2021, he was the writer in residence at the Amy Clampitt House.

ABOUT THE POEMS

This poem contemplates language as much as it contemplates America's obsessive gun culture, finding them tangled up together in surprising ways. The origin of the idiom "to face the music" leads to the memory of a country music festival shooting and the predictably impotent responses, many of which rely on formulaic expressions, snark, or hashtags. This cultural script has begun to feel so inevitable that the poem embodies such inevitability in its prosody: while the odd lines can be composed of any number of syllables (except seven), the even lines are invariably composed of seven syllables. The poem also suggests this functional reticence is hardly disinterested: the less we talk about the real horror of our collective gun violence complacency, the more someone somewhere profits from it—or so the last line supposes. In the end, the poem presents no solutions: solutions belong to policy, not to poetry.

Get Better or Give Up

What follows is a selection of poems protesting the way in which some literary magazines seek to control the poetry marketplace—by refusing to publish poems that have appeared previously on social media.

There is really no excuse for this rule, especially if the mag editors can bring themselves to understand that they created the demand for this alternate publication route by their own long delays in responding to submissions. We have written about this before, in "On Editing: A Modest Proposal for Poetry Magazines" at

https://www.ninemile.org/post/on-editing-a-modest-proposal-for-poetry-magazines.

Many magazines hold submissions for six or seven months to a year or longer. We at *Nine Mile* view this not as fastidiousness but as disqualifying incompetence. As we said in that essay,

> *If seven months is your idea of good editorship,*
> *then let me say again: Go do something else.*
> *Really. Become a trash collector, or house painter,*
> *where the object of your attention is limited to a*
> *single object for a specified period of time, and you*
> *get to go home at night and not worry about*
> *tomorrow until tomorrow; but get the hell out of*
> *editing.*

The result of this incompetence is a burgeoning market in sharing on social media, because poets are not hermits; they write to share, not to gloat Golem-like over the ring of their production. Ruling that such sharing disqualifies the poem for the magazine publication is a way of claiming that the market belongs only to the magazines, and their editors, and to no one else.

What's the next step in this step into Big Brother-control—refuse unpublished work that's been included in a poetry reading? Refuse if the author has shown the work to another, or read it in a class? What is gained by such practice? How is the audience helped, or the authors, or the readers?

Many magazines now allow dual submissions as a way of balancing their extensive delays in responding to submissions. This of course does not solve the problem, it merely shares the strongarming tactic with other magazines.

The solution to the problem is to end the delays in responding to submissions. Back in the day, *The New Yorker* used to respond within a week or two. (The joke was that we put our poems in the mailbox to send to *The New Yorker* and found the rejection slip in the mailbox by the time we got home.)

That can happen again. If not *Nine Mile*'s week or two timeline for response, then it should no take more than a month. In the essay mentioned above, we said,

> *I believe that many magazines treat authors like cattle: Let them wait in line chewing their cuds for their little bit of attention, that may come in a month, two months, seven months, and then give them an acceptance, or reject them in a form letter.*
>
> *After so much delay, even acceptance feels like an afterthought, like O yeah, about your poems...*
>
> *This is scandal, and frankly, it is inexcusable. Either poetry is a great art practiced by people who mean it, or it is the equivalent of doodling on paper during too long committee meetings, distractions from distraction, so that no one, least of all editors, has to take it seriously.*

*"Seriously," in these terms, means that you
accept that the sender of the work is a professional,
who has labored to create the work, and has sent it
to your publication, which he or she respects, in
order to share it with the world in a proper and
appropriate home.*

*Respect to such an author—and we assume that
all authors are like this—means that the author gets
a decision quickly, which means in a week if
possible, and no more than a month if not.*

*If that's not what you believe, then why are you
editing a poetry magazine? Your ethos is that the
publication of such work is important, but your
practice insults your ethos.*

Publication is important. Audience is important. And
authors are important. Editors are not saving poetry by
imposing a gag order constricting where an author can show or
share his or her work. They're not helping their own journals
by doing this. They should recognize this practice for what it
is: a pettiness.

Sam Pereira

Thoughts on Publication & Copyright in 21st Century America

Most of the friends I have here on Facebook and other social media are either writers and/or teachers. So I doubt there will be anyone out there reading this that can't understand what I am about to delve into for a bit.

For over half a century now, I have done my art, in poetic form mostly, and for most of that time I have followed the usual "approved" way of going about the publication of my work. I have been relatively successful in that regard, and I am grateful to the many editors over the years who have chosen to put my stuff in their journals and magazines.

However, in recent years there has evolved a kind of strongarming of the rights of the writer by more than a few editors—not all, thank goodness—saying that if a writer places his or her work online (Facebook, to be specific) then that constitutes "publication," and will not be entertained for possible inclusion in their specific magazines.

Look, I take publication—print or online—by a generally agreed upon actual "publisher" (*Kenyon Review* or *The New Yorker*, let's say) to be considered legitimate, but Facebook is a social media repository that is not and never should be thought of as a literary journal. Your laughter here proves my point, yes.

I place my work online a lot, usually for less than 24 hours, to get some kind of reaction to it, either pro or con, and then I remove it and maybe alter it somewhat, with hope of having it taken by a magazine later, where there is NO confusion about "publication;" then later on maybe, including that work in a book, if I am to be so lucky.

Admittedly, I am old school, but I just don't believe magazine editors, some of whom are my friends, have any right to issue what amounts to a gag order on work that belongs to the writer, while they spend months—and in some cases years—deciding whether they are interested or not. I'm 73 years old now. I haven't got the time to sit around while they lunch over beers and nachos, feeling superior over the approaches a working creative writer may take to move his or her work along in an already difficult system.

I know that I am, no doubt, pissing off some powerful folks with these musings, but I will continue to place poems here [on Facebook] when I feel the need. If there is something I feel has a chance of being accepted by one of the big guns of paper media, then I will send it to them first, fully expecting to wait the usual 12-18 months for a reply. A reply that will most often be "no thanks."

As always, these are MY words; MY thoughts. I do not intend them to be taken by anyone reading them to be a manual on how to handle your own approaches. I hope some of you out there will understand how a poet of some minor repute sees some of these "rules" as bullying on the part a certain segment of the literary publishing industry in its continuing attempt to enforce what amounts to a misrepresentation of America's copyright laws.

Bottom line: In my opinion, putting a creative piece on Facebook, is no different than reading from new unpublished work at a reading in let's say New York City. You come home after, and the next day maybe you decide to send it to one of the big boys. It's what a world that truly loves poetry and free thought should always be espousing.

Respectfully,

Sam Pereira

An Explanation about the Placement of My Work

If I'd waited for the *New Yorker*
To ply me with checks; if I'd stooped
To pick an old poem of mine out of the drink,
And decided to recycle it under the stars
Of an infamous midwestern bar at midnight;

If the editors of *The New York Times* called me
During the middle of dinner, saying how pleased
They'd be to wrap their hands around my insights,
I'd still be doing it the same: letting it out

To the general static of my neighbors; waiting
For honest reactions in the streets. I complain at times
About the swiftness in the lack of thought
Spent disavowing art. I say to those who insist
On thinking their imprimatur makes the difference

As to whether and when I sup on pink meats, or
The gelatinous swill inside the late-afternoons
Of city rains; all tonics and gin a la Billy Joel.
Maybe a man just goes away on tour with the roaches,
And one day is found under a crusted blanket,
Expressing his sins to the penultimate cold.

I write, and most times that suits me. It's enough,
Until a group shows up on my badly peeling porch;
Questioning my sanity and wanting to know why.

Ralph James Savarese

Reputable Poets

Reputable poets do not post unpublished poems on Facebook.
—Private message from a poesy careerist

For Sam Pereira

Think of them as parents who won't
acknowledge the existence of their child
until the child has gotten into Harvard.
Only then do they grant the not so
little shit the status of son or daughter.

Only then do they stuff their pride into
a digital baby carriage and parade it
before the world. "Have you seen my boy
Chester?" Isn't my girl Emeline adorable?"
Cigars for everyone. Champagne, too.

A shower delayed will become a storm.
The umbilical cord, having been cut,
remains attached to the poem. It's like
a Burmese Python in the Everglades
eating you out of house and harm.

Soon, the governor of emotion will have
to sponsor a contest: who can catch
the most resentment? (It, too, is
an invasive species.) Bloated with need,
the poem screams, "So, now I'm worthy?

Watch me drop out of that hipster

finishing school, the *Paris Review*. I'll land
like an asteroid on your cozy den." Poor
thing, it's never been kissed on the head.
It's never had its diaper changed.

Say hello to the honorable Caspar Hauser,
a professional wild child who grew
up in a desk drawer or computer file.
How dismal it was! He carries his father's
name and appears on the man's CV.

Stephen Kuusisto

Publishing Poems on the Internet

—for Ralph Savarese and Sam Pereira

Staid Ianthe unbuttons for me
Though I don't subscribe to *Poetry;*
Here's Childe Harold "refreshed"

(The mode is attic—not so much
Of fashion, misbehaved but touched)
The old girl says a poem is where

We find it…We looked in the reviews,
Found a few quirts to approve,
Short poems as Poe would have them—

We were "turned on" and juicy
Like any reader who's sappy
But most of the stuff was, well

You know—earnest, too steady
For joy—childish, wanting concurrence
Which, as Byron understood

Will ruin the dinner party
"And yet methinks the older that one grows
Inclines us more to laugh than scold, though laughter

Leaves us so doubly serious thereafter."
The little magazines are a drear matter
No amusements there; no champagne no lobster

As Ianthe puts it, and her sisters
Agree, water logged though they are
Drowning beats a moistureless journal…

Bill Schulz

in those days posting poems felt dirty but good

assonance slamming
the random caeusura
flashing tercets
quintains and quatrains

you've reached an unlisted
IP address leave a verse
(nubilous as a Copenhagen
curtain written on your

dandy Tandy TRS-80
shouting o alta vista o
netscape and the rooms the
rooms of America online!)

and we'll get back to you
as soon as we can in those
days we burned our honor-
ariums down at the courthouse

kept envois in our pajama
pockets and posting poems
felt dirty
but good

Andrea Scarpino

Respectable Poets: A Discussion

1.

Respectable poets, they do share
Their verse on Facebook, without a care
For the judgment and critique, that may ensue
Their poetry a source of truth, for all to view

They do not hide, behind closed doors
Their art a source of pride, and not a chore
To share with the world, on social media's shore
Their poetry a source of beauty, for all to adore

Respectable poets, they embrace the change
In how we consume and share, poetry and its range
They adapt and evolve, with the times we arrange
Their poetry a source of hope, in a world that is strange

So let us appreciate and respect
These brilliant wordsmiths, who do not neglect
To share their art, on the virtual stage
Respectable poets, their verse a source of age-old sage

2.

Respectable poets, they do not post
Their verse on Facebook, they do not boast
Of their talent and skill, on social media's coast
They let their poetry, speak for itself and engross

They do not seek fame, or a quick fix
Their art is not for sale, or a simple mix
Of likes and comments, a fleeting thrill

Their poetry's purpose, is to inspire and fulfill

Respectable poets, they are not swayed
By the constant need, to be in the fray
They do not seek validation, from the virtual fray
Their poetry a source of pride, in their own way

So let us appreciate and respect
These brilliant wordsmiths, who do not neglect
Their art for the sake of attention and fame
Respectable poets, their verse remains untamed.

(Note: writtten on ChatGBT)

Jody Stewart

And So It Goes . . .

It was a glorious snow!
And I told

everyone so on Face Book,
that alternate ear.

One grey branch, snow's
delicate ruff on bark, a bit

of intuitive art for friends
before page. Oh, but now,

that small poem's crumpled
in oblivion's cage.

George Drosdowich

The Buffalo

You can't send the Buffalo a poem anymore
They won't take it if you put it on the internet first
Virgin poems only
Even if on your wife's Facebook page
Squiggling like a maiden
A wanted poster for sex
Or the latest boyish indiscretion on Instagram
Verboten!
Bukowski writing on his underwear
The Buffalo don't want it
Even if you have stretched the ass
Of the dead from Manahawkin to Milwaukee
The Sacred Buffalo won't accept it
They don't want to feed the Crow
"Nevermore" anymore
Nor blacken the sky in their mad runs
They aspire to nickels
Standing alone in the snow
Patches of hide on the barbed wire
Dignified resolute reserved fenced-off
Forgotten

Bill Burtis

Measures

Small birds chirping
where this man walks the streets
in his northern city. They are
out of place or character
in January's gloom. The man
stops to listen. He hears
footsteps approaching

where no one appears.
The dull afternoon descends.

The man shrugs, continues
alert now to the sounds
of the birds, footfalls. Perceives
also the hum of a great breathing
he thinks must be the city itself
but realizes this, too, as a new

sensation, filling him slowly

as water, cold and with a pressure
that pushes against that fiber
of his being all those old dreads
push against. He stops again
to take the measure
of what is overtaking him. He looks

up and down the sidewalk, the urge

to get off this street suddenly
expanding within him. He tries
door after locked door. He sees
the light of a café on the corner
but reaching it finds it empty
also locked. He bangs on the glass.

On the sidewalk, in yellow chalk,
someone has left markings
that might have been words
or a sketch of some kind
the many feet of the city have
scuffed into indecipherable swirls.

The chalk lies among the roots of a tree
by the curb; the man takes it,
kneels and begins tentatively
to embolden the images
he thinks he sees in the yellow
eddies of the artist before him.

The cold of the sidewalk
soaks into his knees.
Above him small birds
in an otherwise empty sky.

Robert Desnos

Born in Paris in 1900, Desnos's joined the Dada group in 1919, becoming friends with Andrew Breton, who called him, in the first *Surrealist Manifesto*, the group's "prophet."

Like many other French poets, he and Breton fell out, to such an extent that he joined with other authors to sign *Un Cadaver* (A Corpse) which attached Breton as "Breton the Ox" or "Breton the Oaf."

He became friends with Picasso, Hemingway, Artaud, and John Dos Passos, and wrote on many subjects in many forms, including novels, a play, and a film script, in addition to his several books of poetry. He was active in the French Resistance during WWII, and was arrested by the gestapo on February 22, 1944, and deported to the concentration camps at Auschwitz, Buchenwald, and finally to Terezín, where he died of typhoid a month after the camp's liberation.

He was a prolific author, publishing fourteen books between 1924 and 1945, with another 17 books since. The works selected here are from various periods in his life.

The Watchman of Pont-au-Change (1942)

I am the watchman of the rue de Flandre,
I watch while Paris sleeps.
To the north distant fires light the night.
I hear planes fly over the city.

I am the watchman of Point-du-Jour.
The Seine nestles in shadows behind the Auteuil viaduct,
Under twenty-three bridges across Paris.
To the west I hear bombs exploding.

I am the watchman of the Porte Doree.
The Bois de Vincennes thickens its darkness around the castle.
I have heard screams in the direction of Créteil
And trains roll east with a wave of defiant songs.

I am the watchman of the Poterne des Peupliers.
The south wind brings me an acrid smoke,
Uncertain rumors and sounds of dying.
Which fade somewhere in Plaisance or Vaugirard.

South, North, East, West,
It's all the din of war converging on Paris.
I am the watchman of Pont-au-Change
Awake in the heart of Paris, in the growing roar
Where I recognize the panicked nightmares of the enemy,
Victory cries of allies and of the French,
The cries of suffering of our brothers tortured by Hitler's
    Germans.

I am the watchman of Pont-au-Change
Watching not only over Paris tonight,
This stormy night not only over Paris in its fever and fatigue,

But over the whole world that surrounds us and crushes us.
In the cold air all the din of war
Converges on this place where men have lived for so many
    years.

Cries, songs, groans of the dying, crashes from everywhere,
Victory, pain and death, sky the color of white wine and tea,
From the four corners of the horizon, through all the obstacles
    of the globe,
With scents of vanilla, of wet earth and blood,
Of salt water, gunpowder and funeral pyres,
Kisses from an unknown giant sinking at each step into the
    earth greasy with human flesh.

I am the watchman of Pont-au-Change
And I greet you, at the threshold of the promised day
All of you comrades of the Rue de Flandre to the Poterne of
    the Peupliers,
From Point-du-Jour to the Porte Doree.

I greet you who sleep
After the dangerous clandestine work,
Printers, bomb carriers, rail destroyers, arsonists,
Distributors of leaflets, smugglers, messengers,
I salute you all of you who resist, twenty-year-olds with smiles
    like spring
Old men older than bridges, robust men, images of the
    seasons,
I greet you at the threshold of the new morning.

I greet you on the banks of the Thames,
Comrades of all nations present at the rendezvous,
In the old English capital,
In old London and old Britain.

Americans of all races and flags,
Beyond the Atlantic,
From Canada to Mexico, from Brazil to Cuba,
Comrades from Rio, Tehuantepec, New York and San
    Francisco.
I have made a meeting with the whole world here on the Pont-
    au-Change.
Watching and fighting like you. Just now,
Warned by his heavy steps on the pavement,
I too have slain my enemy.

He died in the gutter, an anonymous and hated Hitler German,
Face stained with mud, memory of him already rotting,
While already I could hear your voices from the four seasons,
Friends, friends and brothers of friendly nations.
I listened to your voices in the scent of African orange trees,
In the heavy smells of the Pacific,
White squadrons of outstretched hands in the dark,
Men from Algiers, Honolulu, Tchoung-King,
Men from Fez, Dakar and Ajaccio.

Intoxicating and terrible clamor, rhythms of lungs and hearts,
From the Russian front blazing in the snow,
From Lake Ilmen to Kief]v, from the Dnieper to Pripet,
You reach me, born from millions of breasts.

I listen to you and hear you. Norwegians, Danes, Dutch,
Belgians, Czechs, Poles, Greeks, Luxembourgers,
Albanians and Yugoslavs, comrades in struggle.
I hear your voices and I call you,
I call you in my language known to all
A language that has only one word:
Freedom!

And I tell you I'm watching and I shot down one of Hitler's
men.
He died in the empty street
In the heart of the impassive city I avenged my brothers
murdered
At Fort de Romainville and Mont Valérien,
In the fleeting and resurgent echoes of the world, the city and
the seasons.

And others than me watch like me and kill,
Like me they watch for the sound of footsteps in deserted
streets,
Like me, they listen to the calls of war and thunder of earth.
At the Porte Doree, at Point-du-Jour,
Rue de Flandre and Poterne des Peupliers,
Throughout France, in towns and fields,
My comrades watch for footsteps in the night
And soothe their loneliness with the rumors and thunder of
earth.

For the earth is a camp lit with thousands of fires.
On the eve of the battle we bivouac all over the land
And perhaps, comrades, you also hear the voices,
The voices that come from here when night falls,
That tear at lips eager for kisses
That fly long across great expanses
Like migratory birds blinded by beacon lights
Smashing themselves into the windows of the fire.

May my voice reach you
Warm and joyful and resolute,
Without fear and without remorse
May my voice reach you with that of my comrades,
The voice of ambush vanguard of France.

Listen to us in your turn, sailors, pilots, soldiers,
We say hello,
We speak not of our sufferings but of our hope,
On the threshold of the new morning we bid you good
    morning,
You who are near and also you
Who will receive our morning greeting
When the early dawn enters your house in straw boots.

Good morning just the same, and good morning for tomorrow!
Good morning with a full heart and with all our being!
Good morning Good morning, the sun is rising over Paris,
Even if the clouds hide it, it will be there,
Good morning Good morning with all my heart Good
    morning!

from *A La Mystérieuse*

No, love is not dead (1926)

No, love is not dead in this heart and these eyes and this mouth
     that has proclaimed its own funeral which is already begun.
Look, I've had enough of quaintness and color and charm.
I love love, its tenderness cruelty.
My love has only one name, one form.
Anything goes. Mouths stick to this mouth.
My love has only one name, one form.
And if some day you remember
O you, that are the form and name of my love,
One day on the sea between America and Europe,
As the sun's final ray reverberates on the undulating surface of
     the waves, or during a stormy night under a tree in the
     countryside, or in a fast automobile,
A spring morning on Boulevard Malesherbes,
A rainy day,
At dawn before you go to bed,
Tell yourself, as I command you familiar ghost to do so, that I
     was the only one to love you so much and it is a pity that
     you never knew it.
Tell yourself to have no regrets: Ronsard and Baudelaire
     before me sang the regrets of the old and dead who despised
     the purest love.
As for you, when you are dead
You will still be beautiful and desirable.
I will be long dead, enclosed entirely within your immortal
     body, in your astonishing image that stands forever among
     the perpetual marvels of this life and eternity,
But if I live
Your voice and its tone, your gaze and the radiance of your
     gaze,

Your fragrance and the perfume of your hair and many other
    things will still live in me,
And I will live too, I who am neither Ronsard nor Baudelaire,
But who am Robert Desnos, who for having known and loved
    you,
Will be no less worthy than them;
I, Robert Desnos, a man who wants to be remembered
For nothing else on this vile earth but his love of you.

Tour of the Tomb

By dint of loving, I lost myself in the ocean.
And what an ocean!

A storm of laughter and tears.

If you board a ship, take care to look at the figurehead, which
    stares with eyes eaten away by the swell and the salt water.

But what am I saying?

The spectacles of Love have little interest for me.
I no longer want only to be a sail carried along by monsoons to
    unknown continents where I will find only one person.
The one for which you have the perfect name.

I undress, like an explorer lost on an island, and I stand
    motionless like a figurehead.

Hail to you, sea breeze and to you, desert, and to you,
    oblivion.

I will be forgotten.
Some day, no one will know my name, but I will know her
    name.
One evening, covered in glory and riches, I will return, knock
    at her door, quite naked, but no one will answer, even after
    the door is opened and I appear in her eyes.

I have gained, at least, the sense of perpetuity.
Not that ridiculous one of cemetery concessions.

I wish in vain for the appearance of the guillotines, but I can only offer the bloodthirsty crowds my wish for suicide.

Revolution!
You will shine after my death, on the immense square of white marble covering my immense corpse.

France is a wasp's nest, Europe a rotten field, and the world a peninsula of my conscience.

Fortunately I still have the stars, and the consciousness of my moral greatness opposed to the thousand obstacles that the world sets up against my love.

The Voice of Robert Desnos (1927)

So like the flower and a current of air
flow of water fleeting shadows
the smile glimpsed at midnight on this excellent evening
so like everything like happiness and sadness
it's the midnight past raising its naked body
above belfries and poplars
I summon those lost in the countryside
old corpses young oaks cut down
shreds of cloth rotting on the ground
and laundry drying around the farms
I summon tornadoes and hurricanes
storms typhoons cyclones
tidal waves
earthquakes
I summon smoke of volcanoes and cigarettes
smoke rings of expensive cigars
I summon loves and lovers
I summon the living and the dead
I summon gravediggers I summon murderers
I summon executioners I summon the pilots the masons
the architects
the assassins
I summon the flesh
I summon the one I love
I summon the one I love
I summon the one I love
triumphant midnight spreads its satin wings and alights
on my bed
belfries and poplars bend to my desire

they are collapsing they are collapsing

those lost in the countryside are found by finding me

the old corpses rise again to life at my voice

young oaks cut down are covered with new greenery

the shreds of fabric rotting in the ground and on the ground
   clap at my voice like the banner of revolt the laundry drying
   around the farms is worn by adorable women whom I do not
   adore who come to me who obey my voice who adore me

tornadoes twist in my mouth

hurricanes redden if it is possible my lips

storms rumble at my feet

typhoons if it is possible ruffle me

I receive drunk kisses from cyclones

tidal waves come to die at my feet

earthquakes do not shake me but make everything crumble at
   my command

smoke of the volcanoes clothes me with its vapors

smoke of cigarettes perfumes me

rings of cigar smoke crown me

loves and the love so long pursued take refuge in me

lovers listen to my voice

the living and the dead submit and greet me the first coldly the
   second familiarly

gravediggers abandon the barely-dug graves and declare that I
   alone command their nocturnal labors

assassins salute me

executioners invoke the revolution

invoke my voice

call my name

pilots steer by my eyes

masons are dizzied listening to me

architects leave for the desert

killers bless me

flesh throbs at my call

the one I love isn't listening
the one I love does not hear
the one I love does not answer.

(from Les Ténèbres, 1927)

Ancient Chaos

A stalk stripped of leaves in my hand is the world
The lock closes on the shadow and the shadow puts its eye to
    the keyhole
And here comes the shadow creeping into the room
Here's the beautiful mistress a more carnal shadow even than
    the great bird of white fur lost in blasphemy perched on the
    shoulder of the beautiful incomparable whore who watches
    over sleep
The path suddenly calms waiting for the storm
A green butterfly net falls on the candle
Who are you who takes the flame for an insect
A strange fight between gauze and fire
I'd like to spend the night at your knees
At your knees
From time to time on your dark calm brow despite the
    nocturnal apparitions I put a disheveled strand of hair back
    into place
I will watch the slow swaying of time and your breathing
This button I found on the ground
It is mother-of-pearl

And I'm looking for the buttonhole that lost it
I know your coat is missing a button
On the mountainside the edelweiss withers
The edelweiss that blooms in my dream and in your hands
    when they open

Good morning greetings when drunkenness is common when
    the adolescent river nonchalantly descends the colossal
    marble stairs in a procession of white clouds and nettles

The most beautiful cloud was newly transformed moonlight
and
The tallest tower was covered in diamonds

Good morning greetings to the coal flower the big-hearted
virgin who will put me to sleep tonight
Good morning to the crystal eyes the eyes of lavender with
eyes of gypsum eyes of dead calm eyes of sobbing eyes of
storm

The flame is in my heart and the sun is in the glass
But never again, alas, will we be able to say again
Good morning everyone!
crocodile eyes of crystal nettles
virgin flowers of coal kind-hearted virgin.